D0834527

# Why...

GOD INTERVENES

Oh...

I UNDERSTAND!

WHY A DAY WAS MISSING
WHY HEZEKIAH'S PRAYER WAS WRONG
WHY GOD SENT A WINDOW
WHY GOD SENT THE DOVE
WHY A PONY LED THEM
WHY GOD SENT A CLOUD
WHY THE SWIM COACH SAW A CROSS
WHY THE TASMANIA FLAG WAS SPARED
WHY GOD PROVIDED A WALL (& 11 OTHERS)

DEVERN FROMKE

Copyright ©2008 SHARPER FOCUS
SF ISBN 978-0-936595-23-8

All rights reserved. No part of this book may be reproduced, stored in a retrieval
system, or transmitted in any form, without the written permission of
SHARPER FOCUS PUBLISHING.

Published by SHARPER FOCUS PUBLISHING division of
SURE FOUNDATION CRT
5671 Polk Drive
Noblesville, IN 46062

www.FromkeBooks.com

Distributed by BOOK DEPOT
11298 Old Paths Lane
Shoals, IN 47581-7234

Scripture quotations noted LB are from *THE LIVING BIBLE*. Copyright 1971 by Tyndale
House Publishing. Wheaton, IL. Used by permission.

Scripture quotations noted Msg -*THE MESSAGE,* Eugene Peterson. Copyright 1993, 1994,
1995, 1996 and 2000. Used by permission of NavPress Publishing Group. All rights
reserved.

Scripture quotations noted NASB from the *NEW AMERICAN STANDARD BIBLE*.
Copyright 1960, 1962, 1963, 1977 by The Lockman Foundation. Used by permission.

Scripture quotations noted NCV are from *THE HOLY BIBLE, NEW CENTURY VERSION*.
Copyright 1987, 1988, and 1991 by Word Publishing, a division of Thomas Nelson, Inc.
Used by permission.

Scripture quotations noted NEB are from *THE NEW ENGLISH BIBLE*. Cambridge: At the
University Press, 1972.

Scripture quotations noted NIV are from the *HOLY BIBLE New International Version*.
Copyright 1973, 1978, and 1984 International Bible Society. Used by permission.

Scripture quotations noted NKJV from the *NEW KING JAMES VERSION*. Copyright 1979,
1980, 1982 by Thomas Nelson, Inc. Used by permission.

Scripture quotations noted Phil are from *THE HOLY BIBLE, PHILLIPS VERSION BIBLE*.
Used by permission of TouchStone Publishing House, New York, NY 10020. All rights
reserved.

CONTENTS

THE PURPOSE OF THIS BOOK

I will never forget when our son (about four years old) was "growing" through his phase of questioning. At times, I must admit, it was a bit tedious, yet I was often impressed that his young mind could encounter such amazing concepts. He almost always began, "Daddy, why . . . ? Why did God make the grass green and the sky blue? Why . . . why . . . ?" And when I offered my best answer, he was so very quick to respond, "OH! . . . Oh!"

Most of us even in our older years continue to ask some difficult "why's." Each of the following lessons will consider a different "why." Above all, we seek to explain why it has been so imperative for God to sovereignly intervene in the affairs of man on planet earth. Here are at least four reasons God intervenes . . .

- to unveil the GLORY OF HIS CHARACTER,

- to magnify the WISDOM OF HIS WAYS,

- to protect the HONOR OF HIS SON,

- to display His DEDICATION TO PURPOSE.

We hope that by the time you have finished reading if you had a "Why?" it has changed to, "OH!" We trust these stories will capture your attention and cause you to enter into His PRIMARY BURDEN in each lesson. As you meditate and prayerfully focus on the Scripture portions we expect God to speak something very personal to you. HE IS A SPEAKING GOD — who really desires our daily participation and fellowship. Only as we wait before Him and ponder His Word can we expect Him to quicken a special word to us for each day.

That the Bible is wholly trustworthy in all its minor details was proven to me one morning as I had finished speaking at a Bible conference in Maryland. A tall, winsome professional man approached me with the statement, "Did you know scientists have now found . . .

WHY A DAY WAS MISSING

I WAS SURPRISED both at his aggressive manner and at the statement. Quite frankly I had not realized there was a missing day but I didn't reveal my ignorance to him.

He proceeded to explain, "I am Harold Hill, president of the Curtis Engine Company in Baltimore. I'm a consultant in the space program." He continued, "One of the most interesting things that God has for us today happened to our astronauts and space scientists at Greenbelt, Maryland. They were checking the position of the sun, moon and planets in space, determining where they would be 100 years and 1000 years from now. This knowledge affects the launching of a satellite in terms of its 'life'. If it's known where the planets are orbiting, the satellite's path can be plotted accordingly.

"The scientists ran the computer measurement back and forth over the centuries and it came to a halt. The computer stopped and picked up a red signal which meant there was something wrong either with the information fed into it or with the results as compared to the standards. The service department was called in to check; they insisted the equipment was perfect.

"The computer operations aide questioned, 'What's wrong?'

"'Well, we have found there is a day missing in space in elapsed time,' was the response as the scientists scratched their heads. There seemed to be no answer.

"One religious fellow on the team stated, 'You know, one time I was in Sunday school when they talked about the sun standing still.'

"The others didn't believe him, but also didn't have any other answer so the response was, 'Show us.'

"He got a Bible, turned to the book of Joshua, and pointed out a passage that seemed pretty ridiculous for anyone with common sense. It began with the Lord saying to Joshua, *'Do not fear them, for I have delivered them into your hand; not a man of them shall stand before you.'* (Josh. 10:8 NKJV) Joshua was concerned because he was surrounded by the enemy and if darkness fell, he would be overpowered. So Joshua asked the Lord to make the sun stand still. That's right! . . . *so the sun stood still in the midst of heaven, and did not hasten to go down for about a whole day.* (vs. 13 NKJV)

"The space scientists exclaimed, 'There is the missing day!' Well, they checked the computers going back into the time it was written and found it was close, but not close enough. The elapsed time that was missing back in Joshua's day was twenty-three hours and twenty minutes . . . not quite a whole day. Rechecking the Bible revealed the significant words, '*about* (approximately) *a day.*' These little words in the Bible are very important.

"But still there was trouble; if forty minutes could not be accounted for, it could cause difficulties 1,000 years from now. Forty minutes had to be found in order to keep it from multiplying many times over in orbit.

6

"Well, this religious fellow also remembered something in the Bible about the sun moving backwards. The scientists remained skeptical about this too; but sure enough, there it was in 2 Kings 20. Hezekiah on his deathbed was visited by the prophet Isaiah and told he was going to die. Hezekiah could not accept this so he prayed for healing. When it was granted, Hezekiah asked for a sign as proof. Isaiah asked, 'Do you want the sun to go ahead ten degrees?'

"Hezekiah replied, 'It's nothing for the sun to go ahead ten degrees, but let the shadow return backward ten degrees.' Isaiah spoke to the Lord, and the Lord brought the shadow ten degrees backward.

"Ten degrees is exactly forty minutes. Twenty-three hours and twenty minutes in Joshua plus forty minutes in 2 Kings make up the missing twenty-four hours the space researchers had to reckon with in their log book as the missing day in the universe."

My friend, Harold Hill, has now gone to his heavenly reward. One day when we discussed this incident he smiled and confided, "Of course the space program has since denied this ever took place, but I was there and vouch that it actually did happen." It is our purpose in the following lessons to discover God's fingerprints in all His interventions. God will verify that His word is exact in every "jot and tittle" — even when there is much enmity in this world seeking to ignore or deny it.

A watch repairman was once asked about a refurbished timepiece, "Now will it keep perfect time?"

The wise repairman astutely replied, "It will keep <u>accurate</u> time, which is all you need. The only thing that keeps perfect time is God's universe. If it did not, everything in orbit would in be total confusion."

HOW WONDERFUL AND EXACT IS GOD'S WORD:

- Matt. 5:18 *For verily I say unto you, Till heaven and earth pass away, one jot or one tittle shall in no wise pass from the law, till all be fulfilled.* (KJV)

- Psalm 19:1-5 *The heavens are telling the glory of God, they are a marvelous display of His craftsmanship. Day and night they keep on telling about God. Without a sound or word, silent in the skies, their message reaches out to all the world . . . The sun lives in the heaven where God placed it and moves out across the skies as a bridegroom going to his wedding . . .* (LB)

- Psalm 119:96-100 . . . *Nothing is perfect except Your words. Oh how I love them. I think about them all day long. They make me wiser than my enemies, because they are my constant guide. Yes, wiser than my teachers, for I am ever thinking of Your rules. They make me even wiser than the aged.* (LB)

It is wonderful to scientifically prove that God's word is trustworthy and also to demonstrate how this created universe is exactly in accord with every detail of God's Word.

What else does God's Word reveal about the missing day? In the story of Joshua's battle with the Amalekites, Joshua prevailed in the battle as long as Moses lifted up his hands in prayer on the mountain. We need to recognize there were two battles raging that day; one was below, on the battlefield as Joshua fought head-to-head with the enemy and the second

8

was above on the mountain as Moses held up the rod of God's authority over the scene below.

Do you recall how Aaron and Hur held up Moses' arms when he became weary? In this role they were obediently functioning as priests assigned by God. It was their interceding that brought victory for Joshua and the army.

God's Word reminds us . . . *when the enemy comes in like a flood, the Spirit of the Lord will lift up a standard against him.* (Isa. 59:19 NKJV)

NOW WE CAN SHARE IN THIS BURDEN: We are all facing a very dark hour. Men with much discernment are predicting that all of Europe will be overrun with Islamic dominance in a very short time. God's warriors must be quick to accept the challenge to stand with God for His purpose if we expect this enemy to be overpowered. Though others may seem indifferent in responding, this should not hinder us from accepting the burden to intercede. This is a most critical hour — time for another sovereign intervention. We must take a stand like Aaron and Hur, expecting God to give victory. Each lesson in this book should awaken you to become God's "standard He is lifting up against the Enemy."

_____

_____

_____

_____

_____

_____

Adapted from a booklet by kind permission of Harold Hill.

How should King Hezekiah have prayed when he received word that he was going to die? Many Bible students have considered this dilemma. King Hezekiah reigned as one of the best kings of Judah: he brought revival, restored temple worship, and trusted God in battle. Yet while receiving this high acclamation we also see . . .

WHY HEZEKIAH'S PRAYER WAS WRONG

IT HAS REMAINED A MYSTERY to Bible students how King Hezekiah could receive the commendation as one of the best kings to reign in Judah and yet miss God's way. In 2 Kings 18 we read, *He trusted in the Lord God of Israel, so that after him was none like him among all the kings of Judah, nor any that were before him . . . and the Lord was with him and he prospered . . .* (5, 7 KJV) In spite of this there is a final dark chapter we need to consider though it is most painful and puzzling.

Without any warning Hezekiah was stricken very suddenly with a serious terminal illness. The prophet Isaiah approached him with this pronouncement, *" . . . set thine house in order; for thou shalt die and not live."* (2 Kings 20:1 KJV)

How does Hezekiah respond? We read in 2 Kings 20:3 that immediately he turned his face to the wall and prayed, *" . . . O Lord, remember now how I have walked before Thee in truth and with a perfect heart, and have done that which is good in Thy sight." And (he) wept sore. (KJV)*

Of course we commend his prayer and weeping; we would expect this from a Godly king. Yet we are very disappointed when we listen closely to his self-relating prayer — his rehearsing before God all he has done. He is reminding God of his own goodness . . . and (perhaps indicating) that this ill treatment of him is not right. Surely this is his own perception of his service, yet Hezekiah's heart is really exposed. Is he implying that God is not really fair? While he does not exactly say it, we sense he is offended that he should receive such treatment.

Before we consider how Hezekiah should have prayed, let us observe how Moses responded when God spoke to him at the burning bush. Humbled and broken after forty years in God's schoolroom, God was now calling Moses to deliver His people out of Egypt. Through his lowly job of tending sheep, God had taught him lessons of humility. Moses displayed this by giving God a dismal review of his shortcomings, not a resume of his glorious achievements (Ex. 3-4).

We wonder — how should Hezekiah have prayed? It is a natural reaction that those who face death are often preoccupied with themselves. They question why this is happening to them. What wrong have they done that needs correction? They question whether their illness is from God or from the devil. But we are disappointed! I believe Hezekiah should have cried out, "Not my will, but Thine be done." If God is through with him, then he must submit and accept this as God's final word spoken through the prophet Isaiah.

When we look for a prayer-pattern, we recognize how our Lord Jesus prayed as He faced death on the cross, *"My Father, if possible let this cup pass from Me. Yet not what I will, but what You will."* (Matt. 26:39 NEB)

If Hezekiah was looking from God's perspective, he could have asked, "What will be best for Your people? How can Your purpose for the nation of Judah be fulfilled?" Instead, Hezekiah was preoccupied with himself and held a private pity-party.

It is a sad story! God did honor Hezekiah's plea for healing; his life and reign were extended for fifteen more years. When the king asked for a sign that this healing would happen, we know that God caused the sun dial to go backwards ten degrees which meant forty minutes were extended to that day.

Amazing! This was another sovereign intervention in which the Creator was dealing with time. In this instance, God added forty minutes to a day, almost as difficult as "causing the sun to stand still *about a day.*"

Consider, though, the tragedy of this wrong prayer — the remaining fifteen-year reign of Hezekiah. History records his many mistakes: (a) He fathered a son whose wicked ways became a disgrace. (b) Hezekiah pridefully and unwisely exposed all the gold and riches of his kingdom to the Assyrian king — who then decided he would invade Judah and take these riches for himself. (c) He responded selfishly, *"Good is the word of the Lord . . . for there shall be peace and truth in my days"* (Isa. 39:8 KJV), when the prophet Isaiah warned him of the consequences of his foolishness. Again, we recognize his concern was primarily for himself, not for the good of God's people.

WHY DID GOD INTERVENE? It is difficult for us to conceive of any good coming from this extension of the king's life. Quite boldly we must write that Hezekiah was "a king who lived beyond God's purpose." Could this be a lesson for all generations to beware of asking God to extend their lifetimes beyond fulfilling His purpose?

WAS THIS INTERVENTION IMPERATIVE? Now 2,500 years later, although we do not presume to question God's wisdom, many are still asking, "Why?" Why this most unusual intervention? Is God speaking to our space-age scientists? God is surely demonstrating the exactness of His timing. The clock of the universe is intricately set. When the sun stood still for "about a day," the time measured twenty-three hours and twenty minutes. In reversing the sun dial of Ahaz, God was now adding another forty minutes to make up a full twenty-four hour day. Amazing indeed how we see God's fingerprints in every part of His creation.

God has always been jealous that His people should have a righteous king, one who would above all acknowledge Him as the King of Kings. Surely He is speaking to all generations reminding us that above all else, we must seek for His purposes to be fulfilled. We agree with Samuel the prophet, *As for God, His way is perfect* . . . (2 Samuel 22:31 NKJV)

WE PRAY: Father / God . . . it is so evident that You seek for us to be one with Your purpose and Your ways.

_____

_____

_____

_____

_____

_____

Diagram of Hezekiah's sundial by James Seward

IT WAS THE DIVINE IMPERATIVE. From the beginning, all mankind has desired a look at the God of the Universe. In recognizing this, historians have written about "the desire of all nations". So in the "fullness of time" God sent His Son.

WHY GOD SENT HIS WINDOW

WHEN JORDAN FINISHED HIS EVENING PRAYER, he looked up at his mother and sighed, "It surely would be a lot easier to pray if God would just open up His window in heaven and show His face. Then we would know for sure He is there — and what He looks like."

With much motherly wisdom she answered, "Oh, God did something better than that in sending His son, Jesus. He is like a window, helping us see what God is like."

When Jesus came to earth He announced that He had come to show us the Father. When Philip wanted to see God, Jesus said to him, "When you see Me you see My Father." So Jordan is like most of us who really want to see and know God better. While it is most important that Jesus came to be our Savior from sin, He also came to give us a better understanding of the nature and character of God the Father.

Through the years I have attempted to use a simple diagram to explain God. I have drawn a rough sketch which illustrates WHAT GOD IS . . . (His natural attributes) and WHAT GOD DOES . . . (His moral attributes, e.g., character).

One day I was explaining how a diamond with its many facets can illustrate God's attributes. A jeweler friend suddenly exploded with much enthusiasm. With his pen he quickly sketched a diamond, explaining how some diamonds have a <u>window</u> through which one can see the various facets of the jewel. I have never forgotten his excitement as he emphasized the uniqueness and importance of the window.

<u>What God Does</u>

1. Creates
2. Rules
3. Provides
4. Redeems
5. Sanctifies
6. Begets
7. Sustains

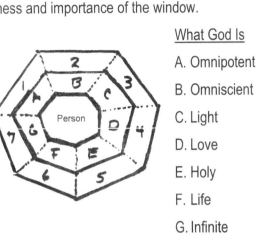

<u>What God Is</u>

A. Omnipotent
B. Omniscient
C. Light
D. Love
E. Holy
F. Life
G. Infinite

This sketch of a diamond shows the window with its many facets. In the outer circle, we see God's activity, listing just a few of His more important works. God creates, rules, provides, redeems, sanctifies, begets and sustains; these are usually referred to as the moral attributes. In the next circle, we consider what God is in His nature and name just a few of His more important characteristics. God is omnipotent, omniscient, life, light, love, infinite and holy — usually called the natural attributes.

If you are questioning why we spend time considering these simple aspects of theology, let me illustrate. Dr. Mark Bubeck explains the necessity of helping children (like Jordan) and immature believers avoid foolish praying. He elaborates with the following examples: A new believer was learning to pray aloud in a small group. There were the usual pauses, the hesitancy, and the sometimes clumsy effort to say what he desired.

The group struggled to hold back laughter as he closed, "And God, please take care of Yourself, because if anything happens to You, we're all sunk."

And then there was the small child who was about to move to a distant city. The night before their departure he ended his prayer with, "I guess this is goodbye, God, because tomorrow we're moving to Cleveland."

You may smile at this kind of childish foolishness in praying, but there are many other just-as-foolish prayers in which we innocently become involved. So we need to understand the important attributes of God. We need to realize that God is everywhere (omnipresent) and that He is all-powerful (omnipotent). During the years Jesus walked before mankind, He demonstrated all these attributes. What He DID and what He WAS . . . revealed what God the Father is like.

About fifty years ago, people were primarily asking, "Does God exist?" Today that question has changed to, "What is God like and what difference can He make in my life?" Even for many people who have an enormous accumulation of Biblical knowledge, God makes little difference in how they actually live. That is because they know about Him, but have not allowed Him to invade their daily lives.

Even more than we need knowledge about Him, we need to experience Him. How do we do that? We invite Him not merely to indwell us, but to be Lord of our living. If Christ doesn't make any difference in my ethics and values on my job; if He doesn't affect my speech and my attitudes toward co-workers and family; if He makes absolutely no difference in the way I live and work — then, pray tell, what difference does He make? Are we playing a religious game that is all talk and no action? The lessons in this book are focused to help us move into this reality.

So, Jordan, your deep desire to see God was fulfilled. God realized how much all of mankind has longed to see and know Him. Remember, while God's children who believe in the Lord Jesus see the Father <u>now</u>, some day the Father and His family will be on full display for all the world to see. *"Then cometh the end, when He shall have delivered up the Kingdom to God, even the Father . . ."* (1 Cor. 15:24 KJV)

HIS COMING WAS A DIVINE IMPERATIVE: The coming of the Lord Jesus as the Window is surely the ULTIMATE INTERVENTION; it becomes the great pivotal point of all human history. While it is true Jesus came to redeem fallen man, He also came to reveal the Father and His character.

GOD'S WORD EXPLAINS: Philip, voicing the heart-cry of all of us, recognized how important this was when he said, *"Show us the Father, Lord, and we will be satisfied."* (John 14:8 Phil.) Jesus answered him (vs. 9), *"Have I been such a long time with you, without your really knowing Me? The man who has seen Me has seen the Father."*

NOW THIS MUST BECOME OUR BURDEN: Each day we ask the Lord for help in properly representing Him — in the little things, in the ways we respond, and in the reactions we have towards others. Since Jesus was the Window, then we also must become windows. How? We rejoice that God will give special grace for this . . .

WE PRAY: Father, we are so much like Philip . . . and like Jordan. When we would see You, we know You will simply reply, "When you have seen Him, you have seen Me!"

We now consider the coming of the Holy Spirit. Why is this intervention so imperative? Among others, there are the following three reasons: first, the coming of the Spirit proves that Jesus has been seated at the right hand of His Father; second, He has come to reveal and exalt the Lord Jesus; and third, He has come to indwell and enable each believer for special ministry.

WHY GOD SENT HIS DOVE

IT HAS BEEN SAID THAT WHEN THE NORWEGIAN EXPLORER Fridtjof Nansen went to the North Pole in 1893, he took with him a strong, fast, carrier pigeon. As the story goes, after many difficult months of travel, he reached the desolate Arctic region of the North Pole; there he penned a tiny message attaching it to the pigeon. Taking the trembling bird in hand, he flung it upward into the foreboding atmosphere. The bird circled three times and then headed south — 2,000 miles over ice and ocean back to Norway. When the bird finally arrived at the Nansen home, his wife knew her husband had arrived at his North Pole destination.

In a similar manner God has sent His heavenly Dove, the Holy Spirit, as proof that Jesus has arrived and is now seated at the right hand of the Father. As the Father promised, the Spirit, who was poured out upon Christ, has now descended down to the Body below. (Psa. 133)

What a wonderful proof! The Holy Spirit's coming was evidence that Jesus was now seated at His Father's right hand. Jesus said, *"I will pray the Father and He will give you another helper . . ."* (Jn. 14:16 NKJV)

Perhaps the following story, told about two famous men, will help illustrate the importance of the Holy Spirit's coming. According to the narrative, the wind blew fiercely and the rain beat down on a traveler as he lugged two heavy suitcases toward Grand Central station in New York City. At times he would pause to rest and regain his strength before trudging on against the elements. At one point he was almost ready to collapse when a man suddenly appeared by his side, took the suitcases, and said in a strangely familiar voice, "We're going the same way, let me help you."

When they reached the shelter of the station, the weary traveler, the renowned educator Booker T. Washington, asked the helper, "Please sir, what is your name?"

The man replied, "The name, my friend, is Roosevelt — Teddy — many of my friends call me that." And then . . . he was gone! I have often reflected — if this story is true, perhaps Booker enjoyed telling his friends that he had been helped by none other than Teddy, the helper who later became President of the United States.

Thus, we explain the second reason for the Holy Spirit's coming to earth. He came to be our helper — one called alongside — yet something even better. When Jesus was announcing this Helper, He explained that the One who had been <u>with</u> them would now be <u>in them</u> (Jn. 14:17). This was an amazing improvement! In the past the "paracletos" had been with them; now He was to indwell them. It was quite wonderful for Teddy Roosevelt to move alongside as a helper, but how much better if he could have invaded — yes, indwelt Booker?

There is a third reason for the Holy Spirit to come as a Dove. Throughout the Old Testament, men have been mostly occupied with the working of the Spirit such as represented in wind, fire and water. Now, with the coming of the Dove, we are introduced to the person of the Holy Spirit. Remember, in salvation every believer has experienced the work of conviction and regeneration by the Holy Spirit. Yet too often the Spirit has not been honored as a Person who seeks a governmental position of authority in one's life.

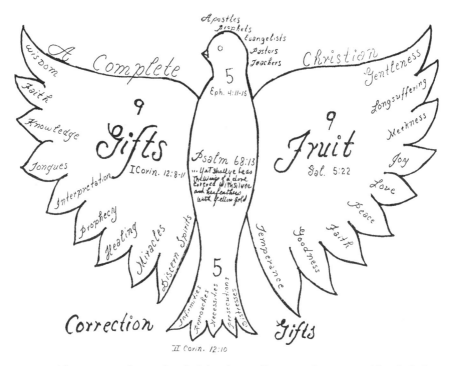

Years ago I received this dove diagram from my friend A.S. Worley. He explains how each dove is uniquely designed, and why this is so significant. Mr. Worley insists that each wing of a dove has nine feathers, nine — no more and no less. He suggests that these feathers picture the nine-fold fruit of the Spirit on one wing, and the nine gifts of the

Spirit on the other wing. He insists this is no coincidence; God has purposely placed nine feathers on each wing of the dove. In the picture we have designated a label for each feather on the wings and also the five feathers on the tail.

We would agree that for any bird to function properly both wings are vital. Whoever saw a one winged bird flying very high? So it is with man! When the Holy Spirit comes to dwell within man He will develop character (fruit) in his life, but also enable him to serve (by gifting). Both wings are imperative — character for our inner life and gifting (anointing) for spiritual service.

For many years I pondered the unique plaque on the wall of one of my pastor friends which describes the importance of employing both wings:

WHAT I BUILD WITH MY GIFTEDNESS,
I CAN DESTROY WITH MY CHARACTER.

In the Bible, as well as these present days, we have often observed the tragedy in a man's ministry when moral failures send his building work into disaster (i.e., gifting without character.) But we also recognize that a person may develop character (which is the fruit of the Spirit) yet lack anointing on his gifting, thus producing much limitation (i.e., character without anointing).

God sent His Dove because He knew how imperative it was for every believer to be empowered for a personal walk of holiness as well as to be fully equipped for effective service. It is my prayer that this simple exhortation showing the need and the balance of both wings of the Dove should encourage every reader to recognize that the Dove is not just an enhancement but actually an imperative. Without the Dove fully operational in our lives we are continually <u>victims</u>; God, however, plans for us to be <u>victors</u>!

Charles H. Spurgeon, known as the prince of preachers, felt he had delivered his sermon so poorly one Sunday that he was ashamed. As he walked away from his church, the Metropolitan Tabernacle in London, he wondered how any good could come from that message. Arriving home, he dropped to his knees and prayed, "Lord God, You can do something with nothing; please bless that poor sermon." The following Sunday, to make up for his previous "failure," Spurgeon prepared what he felt was a "great" sermon. Amazingly, over the following months, forty-one different people revealed that because of the "weak" message they had decided to trust Christ as Savior; however, as far as Spurgeon knew, no one at all responded to his "great" message.

It was later that Spurgeon realized, "It was God's anointing that made the difference." God was teaching him the difference between depending on the anointing or his natural abilities. The apostle Paul discovered the same lesson — that our weakness is an occasion for the working of God's power.

Consider the next point. The dove has more than wings; it also possesses a tail and a head. There is spiritual significance in this. Mr. Worley suggests that every dove has five tail feathers — five, no more and no less. He believes this illustrates the Apostle Paul's own testimony of how God used *infirmities, reproaches, necessities, persecutions and distresses.* (2 Cor. 12:10 KJV)

23

Paul recognized these five feathers as correctional gifts which God used to keep his ministry on course. He even learned to take pleasure in them after fervently pleading with God to remove *"this thorn in the flesh"* which was such a bother to him. After his third plea, Paul received the explanation that *My grace is sufficient for you, for My strength is made perfect in (your) weakness.* (2 Cor. 12:9 NKJV)

Now let us consider the importance of the head of the dove. First we recognize that God gives gifts to individuals for personal ministry, but He gives gifted individuals to the church for the directing and building of it. These gifted men He calls apostles, prophets, evangelists, teachers and pastors. This five-fold ministry serves as the headship for His church.

It is very interesting that those who are in leadership will most likely experience correction such as illustrated by the five tail feathers. When you read the life-stories of many of the servant-leaders who have truly counted for God's purposes, you recognize how "tail-feathers" have so often played an important part.

IT IS IMPORTANT TO RECOGNIZE: All believers have the indwelling Spirit from the moment of their believing. But the real question is, "Does the Holy Spirit really have <u>them</u> under His lordship?" Though we may talk much about the Holy Spirit, is He really functioning in a living way in our church body? Is His presence expected and enjoyed in each worship service?

HOW CAN WE SHARE IN HIS BURDEN? There are many real needs in every church body, and in the lives of many folk around us. How can we become the tool God will use? Remember Moses! When he saw their great need, he prayed one thing, ". . . if Your presence

doesn't go with us . . ." This was his primary concern; what else could distinguish Israel from all other people in this world?

Today the church <u>must have His presence</u>! We must no longer take the Holy Spirit for granted. Only as we choose to <u>honor</u> Him as a Person can we expect Him to exalt the Lord Jesus as Head — and it is when we are under His Headship that we enjoy His Presence.

Father, beginning today, please hasten the mighty work of THE DOVE. Let Him invade my life — our lives — and using both wings bring important spiritual fruitfulness and balance.

_____

_____

_____

_____

_____

_____

_____

_____

_____

_____

_____

_____

_____

_____

_____

_____

Picture of the Dove by A.S. Worley, Walhalla, S.C.

Seeing a shadow by the light of the moon changed his life. Was it mere coincidence or was it God's special intervention?

WHY THE COACH SAW A CROSS

BECAUSE HE WAS THE SWIMMING COACH in a large college for men, they were puzzled by his unusual behavior. Each Thursday night as he arrived at the large indoor swimming pool he would go straight to the edge, dip his big toe in the water, and then climb up the highest diving board. Of course, he made a wonderful dive and swam up and down the pool with the best of form. But why would such an expert swimmer resort to such a novice-like habit as sticking his big toe in the pool before swimming? One night they mustered the courage to ask why he went through this strange ceremony.

Smiling, he answered, "Really I suppose it is just a force of habit, but back of it all there is an unusual reason. One night I could not sleep, so I decided to slip into the swimming pool, assuming a bit of exercise would induce the much-needed rest. I did not turn on the pool lights, for I knew every inch of the place. The roof was made of glass and the moon shone through, throwing the shadow of my body onto the wall at the other end. My body with arms extended made a perfect sign of the cross as I stood on the diving board. I cannot explain why I did not dive at that moment; there was no premonition of any kind.

"I was a Christian and as I stood looking at the shadow of the cross, I began to think of Christ hanging on the cross, its meaning and how it truly affected my life. Poised there on the diving board, I cannot say

how long I stood nor why I did not dive. I came down from the board and walked along the pool's edge to the steps leading to its depths; there I began to descend. Reaching the bottom, my feet touched the cold, smooth floor of the pool. It was empty!

"Earlier that evening, the caretaker had drained the pool dry, and I knew nothing about it! I realized then that had I dived, I would have dived to my death. I guess that may explain to you why I always put my toe into the water before diving."

The coach was confident that God had intervened to spare his life, but even more, to awaken him to see a deeper reality of the Cross. For many years he had realized that Christ died as a substitute <u>for</u> him, but that night he was awakened to realize that he had died <u>with Him</u>. As he stood looking at that shadow on the wall he saw not only Christ on the cross, but he saw himself nailed there <u>with Him</u>. It was God's very unique intervention that would forever change his life.

Those who know the personal testimony of four outstanding servants of the Lord will recognize a similar experience when each died to self and sin:

When questioned about his spiritual power, George Müller responded, "One day George Müller died."

D.L. Moody explains how he was visiting in New York City when he "consciously died to his own ambitions".

Charles Finney, the revivalist, whose ministry shook the New England states, told how he slipped away to a secluded spot in the forest where he "died to self."

Christmas Evans wrote about his surrender to Christ, "I gave my soul and body to Jesus which was in a very real sense, 'a death to self.'"

Perhaps these words of John Gregory Mantle summarize the experience best. "There is a great difference between realizing, 'On that cross He was crucified for me,' and 'On that Cross I am crucified with Him.' The first aspect brings us deliverance from sin's condemnation, the second from sin's power."

THE DIVINE IMPERATIVE: What happened to these four men and to the swimming coach should become a personal reality in each of us. From the moment of surrender forward, we must realize "we are as dead men on furlough." Through the blood we have forgiveness, but through the work of the cross, sin should no longer have dominion over us. We have died to our selfish desires, pursuits and appetites in this co-death experience.

There is much more! Each one of us should enjoy the full value of all that Jesus Christ accomplished for us, not only in His

death but also in His resurrection. We are not only dead with Him, but we are also alive with Him — "fully alive unto God" should be our new testimony. The well-known songwriter, D.W. Whittle, describes it thus in his famous hymn, "Moment by Moment":

> Dying with Jesus by death reckoned mine,
>
> Living with Jesus a new life divine.
>
> Looking to Jesus 'til glory doth shine —
>
> Moment by moment, O Lord, I am Thine.

WE PRAY: Father, it is our deepest cry to You that we shall come into the full reality of Your death and resurrection. Make it so from this day onward. Amen!

_____

_____

_____

_____

_____

_____

_____

_____

_____

_____

_____

_____

_____

_____

Picture by James Seward

One morning as we sat at the breakfast table visiting with Mark and Bonnie, I discovered she had come from Swan Quarter, North Carolina. That quaint little town on the coast had captured my attention when Paul Harvey explained on his newscast how a church building actually floated down Main Street. But let me explain from the beginning this story of . . .

WHY THE CHURCH FLOATED

IN THE EARLY DAYS some very earnest believers wished to have a place to worship right in the center of their little town. They diligently asked God to supply the funds to build and then to help them obtain a suitable location on which to erect the building, the latter of which became the focus of their praying.

Finally adequate funds were accumulated and a choice site was agreed upon, right in the middle of the town providing convenience for all members and serving as a lighthouse for the community. Because money was scarce, it was evident that this small building would need to be a very simple wooden structure of the cheapest materials.

When the believers approached Mr. Cash, who owned the desired piece of land on which they wanted to build, they secretly hoped that God would burden him to donate the site for this noble purpose. However the committee appointed to meet with Mr. Cash soon discovered that he had no interest in their venture; in fact, he made it very clear there was no use talking about it. The deed he held stated very clearly that this parcel of land must be neither donated nor sold.

When the committee reported his response to the church you can imagine the disappointment. Many pondered why God had not answered their prayers. They were still convinced that this site was God's intention for them. What had gone wrong? Furthermore, many were dissatisfied with the only other parcel of ground available, which was quite some distance from the town center, and not nearly as desirable.

Soon it was agreed they should wait no longer. The little wood structure was erected on that location where the church body enjoyed much growth and blessing. Yet they continued to question why they had been hindered from securing their original building site.

NOW IT WAS TIME FOR GOD'S INTERVENTION. The God who holds the winds, the seas and the storms in His own hands was about to show His strong arm. Swan Quarter was situated right on the Atlantic sea coast; in its past history fierce squalls had often sent torrents of water rushing down the town's streets. But this storm which was descending upon them brought extra rain and greater flooding. The believers were immediately gripped with great concern for their church building which began to shudder and then rise with the swirling flood waters. It was being lifted from its brick foundation. What would happen? Was this to be the end of their humble little sanctuary?

The scene they were about to see was wholly beyond comprehension! Once the church building was afloat it became a veritable "ark" which slowly moved out into the nearby street. There it was met with a strong current; accompanied by wind, it moved right down the avenue until it came to Main Street. Suddenly, it turned squarely at right angles and headed for the center of Swan Quarter. No one could explain, except that an "unseen pilot" seemed to be giving directions. In fact this "unseen pilot" was steering their building to the very site where it should have been located from the beginning. Yes, believe it or not, that little wooden structure moved more than a

mile and did not stop until it floated directly to that vacant site belonging to Mr. Cash. There it came to rest!

When Mr. Cash observed what had happened, he went immediately to the office of the Town Register of Deeds and turned over the property to the church officers. It was to be his appointment with God! He could not deny this most sovereign intervention. The whole community rejoiced in God's goodness, but even more in His faithfulness to answer their prayers.

CONSIDER THIS DIVINE IMPERATIVE: God is always watching over the integrity of His name and the promises folk may have claimed. Furthermore He is very jealous that His church — those people who represent His name and purpose in a community — be as a Light set upon a hill. Surely this most sovereign intervention was unusual. How shall we understand it?

We must be very clear in understanding what the church really is. Gary Bergel explains, "The church in a Biblical sense never refers to a (physical) facility. In the Old Testament, the Hebrew root word, 'gabal', designates an assembly of God's people who plan or execute war or deliberate to judge. The parallel Greek word, 'ekklesia', indicates a called-out assembly of citizens that discusses and governs the affairs of state."

So, while folks generally refer to the building they attend as a church, it actually is not the place they meet but rather the people with whom they assemble. When Jesus said, *"I will build My church,"* He was not referring to a physical place. Today we are called to preach the Kingdom and disciple nations (ethnos). As we do, Christ will build His Church in His own way.

CAN WE ENTER INTO HIS BURDEN? It is not easy for folk to adjust their thinking. Down through the centuries believers have met in very unusual places such as dungeons, or caves, or homes, or at the seashore. Believers were not as building-conscious as we have become today. We do not ignore the importance of having an adequate meeting place, but I wonder if God's desire to honor this group of believers' prayers was perhaps more important than just moving a building to a central place.

We realize folk will follow their traditions (emphasizing a physical place) until God awakens them to His burden — a living assembly of His people gathered each Lord's Day unto His name for His glory and their mutual encouragement.

WE PRAY: Father/God, Your ways are awesome. Who can ever find them out? Who can understand why You respond to some prayers, yet seem to ignore others! All we know is that You are zealous toward those believing saints who are called by Your name. Because they find their delight in You, You will delight in them. Amen!

_____

_____

_____

_____

_____

_____

_____

_____

_____

_____

_____

_____

_____

_____

_____

_____

_____

_____

_____

_____

_____

Permission to use picture: Harvey & Tait, Yanceyville, NC

Sometimes it seems as though God moves folk around like checkers on the board so that it often seems they have little choice. Yet, their final testimony is "they would have chosen this course — had they known in the beginning." We consider two such and . . .

WHY GOD POSITIONED THE GIRLS

CONSIDER THIS STORY TOLD OF HOW GOD used two orphan girls from Martinique, brought up as Christians, to influence foreign courts and to help decide the destiny of nations. One of the girls relates the following account:

My name is Marie Aimee Dubuc de Rivery; I was born in 1765 in Martinique. I lost both of my parents at a young age, but the gentleman who became my guardian was very kind, giving me the best of care. Josephine, my cousin, was my best friend.

In 1776, I was sent to France to finish my education where my teachers praised my ability as a student. With education behind me, I set out again for my homeland. After a few days of sailing, our vessel was attacked by Algerian Corsairs. They won the fight that ensued, and we passengers of the ship were made prisoners. The old pirate chieftain, attracted by my blue eyes and golden hair, decided to send me as a gift to his master, the Bey of Algiers.

The Bey of Algiers decided to send me as an appeasement gift to the Sultan of Turkey. Accordingly, I was outfitted appropriately for the ruler of the Ottoman Empire and then set sail. During this long voyage, I almost prayed for death. However, a determination would sweep over me to show the infidel Turks what a woman was like who had been brought up under the benefits of Christian civilization. I resolved never to renounce my Christian faith.

Then one day, a vision of golden towers and mosques appeared on the horizon. My voyage was over, and I stood on the brink of a new life. The Sultan accepted me as a gift from the Bey, which renewed and cemented the friendship between the two. My new quarters were in the Seraglio, the Sultan's palace. The Seraglio was a city in itself, capacious enough to house twenty thousand people. I knew the ruler of Turkey held complete sway over his subjects — both body and soul. Nevertheless, I made up my mind that I would rather die than lose my faith in God and be plunged into spiritual darkness.

My son, Mahmud, was born July 20, 1785. His hair and eyes were dark like his father's. How carefully I guarded my little one! As soon as he was old enough to understand, I began to pour into his ears the truths which I had believed all my life.

My guardian finally learned of my whereabouts, and we were able to carry on a correspondence. It was amazing! He told me that my cousin Josephine had married Napoleon Bonaparte and had become the Empress of France.

On July 28, 1808, my son Mahmud became the ruler of Turkey. The spiritual influences which I had conveyed to him from his childhood had by this time become a part of his very being. I knew he would not be the despotic ruler his predecessors had been.

As I thought of Josephine in her high station and of myself in my unbelievable role, a wave of homesickness for our island home swept over me. But I was confident that God had placed each of us in our hidden place of influence. Josephine and I exchanged letters, as our comradeship could only be renewed in this way. Napoleon wrote to Mahmud, desiring his friendship and asking for military aid. Would Mahmud lend him troops for the proposed campaign into Russia?

One day, my son came to me in my garden. He desired advice at this crucial time. We earnestly discussed the matter, walking to and fro along the narrow paths. Napoleon little guessed that the answers to his letters were influenced by a woman. I can truly say that, in the advice I gave, I had the interest of France at heart.

Then word reached me that Napoleon had divorced Josephine. I knew that his action was not right. All my religious teachings of the past rose up in rebellion against it. Mahmud and I again walked in the garden the evening after I had received the sad message, and I confided it to him. He said little, but I know he felt that anything which so hurt his mother was wrong; hence, it was not to be passed over lightly.

Mahmud left me and returned to his room. On the table another communication from Napoleon awaited him. He read it with a frown. Although he had already made a promise, now our talk in the garden stood between him and its fulfillment. "Napoleon has been untrue to my mother's ideals," he thought. "How can I trust him? If I enter into an alliance with him, what may he not do to me?"

And so the promise was never kept. Mahmud did not send troops to aid Napoleon in his Russian campaign. History records the dreadful failure of that campaign. The crestfallen French soldiers, caught in the deadly grip of a Russian winter, struggled to return home as best they could. Thousands of them froze to death. Perhaps, if I had more fully understood the situation, I might have tried to persuade my son to keep his word on this occasion; a promise is a sacred thing. But it is useless to ponder over that now.

I saw many urgently needed reforms accomplished in Turkey through my son. The secret of my influence with him was easily kept because the mother of a sultan is of no apparent consequence whatsoever; indeed, she is considered a slave. Someone, however, who understood the true state of affairs, declared that, "in the recesses of the Seraglio, Mahmud caught a light which had never penetrated there before — the light of Christianity." Historians recognized Mahmud as the only sultan of the Ottoman Dynasty in modern times who possessed the qualities of a great ruler.

HOW CAN WE SHARE IN GOD'S BURDEN? In the Bible there are several examples of God placing someone in a position to influence those of great importance. Consider how Esther was available for *"such a time as this."* **Consider how Abigail turned the heart of David when he was angry with Nabal and how Ruth won the heart of Boaz. Consider Hannah who was barren until God gave her Samuel, a wise prophet for the nation of Israel.**

GOD' S WORD IS CLEAR: *The king's heart is in the hand of the Lord, as the rivers of water: He turneth it whithersoever He will.* **(Prov. 21:1 KJV)**

WE PRAY: Father, help us to accept the low place, to be willing to be hidden. I know You have not called us all to position or success . . . but only to be faithful to our own calling.

FOOTNOTE*: If you wonder whether Josephine might have left any deep impression on her husband, Napoleon, consider this. When Napoleon was banished in exile to the island of St. Helena later in life, he gave himself to studying the Bible and theology. One day he asked his general, Monotholon, "Can you tell me who Jesus Christ is?"

When the general was unable to respond, Napoleon said, "Well, then I will tell you. Across a chasm of 1800 years, Jesus Christ makes a demand which is above all others difficult to satisfy. He asks for that which a philosopher may often seek at the hands of his friends, or a father of his children, or a bride of her spouse. He asks for the human heart. He will have it entirely to Himself. He commands it unconditionally...all who sincerely believe in Him experience that remarkable supernatural love toward Him. This is what strikes most men. I have often thought of it . . . it proves to me quite conclusively the divinity of Jesus Christ."

It seems to many critical observers, that Napoleon's testimony to Christ makes it very clear that at some point he became a Christian.

_____

_____

_____

_____

_____

_____

*Adapted from: "Spiritually Alive" by Dr. D. James Kennedy

God will reveal how much He is concerned as a Father for families. This amazing intervention, passed on from generation to generation, demonstrates . . .

WHY GOD PROVIDED A WALL

A WIDOW WITH THREE CHILDREN was facing a predicament. Word had reached their community that they were right in the pathway of Napoleon's army which was in full retreat. Neighbors were rushing about gathering a few valuables and necessary provisions in wagons, carts or by horseback — any way available to escape from Napoleon's soldiers who had suffered such losses and setbacks that they exercised little discipline. Napoleon himself had already returned to France. So it was every soldier scrounging for himself.

Tales of destruction and cruelty had reached their village long before the foreign army arrived. For that reason every house would be evacuated — that is except for the house of this widow and her children. Little Joseph was a helpless cripple and could not be moved. One moment he would plead with his mother and sisters not to leave him, and the next he would urge them to rush away with the others and not bother about him. But the mother, who loved and trusted her Father above, would not consider his plea.

"We're going to stay and trust Father/God to care for us," she announced firmly. "God will not leave us defenseless." She gathered her little family to her side and prayed before going to bed, "Oh, God build a wall around our home and protect us from the enemy."

As the children crawled into bed, they questioned each other, "What did Mother mean, asking God to build a wall around our house?"

That night as they slept, the cruel enemy passed by their place but the little family neither saw nor heard them. Looking out the windows the next morning, there was nothing visible but a white wall extending straight upwards. Opening the back door leading to the animals' shelter, they saw the only available space in any direction. A shed on the windward side had provided protection leaving an open passageway to the building where their grain, milk and eggs were kept. Otherwise they were completely engulfed.

What had happened? Their little cottage was entirely concealed from view because of a great white wall — a snowdrift which had been building all through the night. <u>Father/God had intervened to protect His family.</u>

In Job 37:6 we read, *He saith to the snow, "Be thou on the earth . . ."* (KJV) Again we read in Psalm 148:8 about the stormy wind fulfilling His will. Using these two servants, Father had built His own sure wall of concealment and protection around this defenseless family.

Why would Father/God show such special goodness to this widow and her family? James reminds us, *Pure religion and undefiled before God and the Father is this, to visit the fatherless and widows in their affliction . . .* (James 1:27 KJV) Just imagine how those children for many years could look back upon the promise their mother had claimed. They could boldly announce that their God was indeed faithful! They could trust both His Word and His character. Yes, this story of awesome intervention has been passed down through several generations who enjoy passing it on.

Consider another "snow" story. The widowed mother of several small children served the last of their meager supply of bread for supper one snowy night. She had no money to buy more and wondered what she would give them to eat for breakfast.

The next morning the table was set as usual and the children called to take their places. Then the mother proclaimed, "Children, we need bread. We must ask the Lord to supply our need." And pray they did . . . all of them. Scarcely had they finished their earnest petitions, when a loud knock at the kitchen door sent the oldest boy running across the room to answer it.

When the door opened, a voice announced, "My truck's stalled in a snowdrift around the corner. I can't make any more deliveries today, and I can't sell this tomorrow. Ask your mother if she can make use of these, Sonny!" Without even waiting for an answer the driver unloaded his arms piled high with fragrant loaves of bread.

There are some requests that are very clearly "will-of-God" praying. Our heavenly Father extends special grace and mercy to widows and orphans. So we can boldly plead this promise, *This is the confidence that we have in Him, that if we ask anything according to His will, He hears us.* (1 Jn 5:14 NKJV)

THIS DIVINE IMPERATIVE in our Father's heart shows His concern for widows and their families. The apostle Paul alerts us to the significance of His Fatherhood . . . *I bow my knees unto the Father of*

(Eph. 3:14-15 KJV)

It becomes very clear why He extends such mercy and grace to widows and orphans. His word exhorts us as follows:

. . . Afflict not a widow . . . (Ex. 22:22 KJV)

. . . He will establish the border of the widow . . . (Prov. 15:25 KJV)

God executes the judgment of the fatherless and widow . . . in giving them food and raiment . . . (De.10:18 KJV)

. . . visit the fatherless and widows in their affliction . . . (James 1:27 KJV)

WE PRAY: Father, it is with such new understanding that we say, Our Father! You are not some distant God in the heavens; You are all that our Lord Jesus said You were. "For the Father Himself loves you, because you have loved Me, and have believed that I came forth from God. I came forth from the Father, and have come into the world. Again, I leave the world and go to the Father." Amen! (Jn. 16:27-28 NKJV)

_____

_____

_____

_____

_____

_____

_____

_____

_____

_____

In this day when men are prone to use themselves and their experiences as touchstones, it is necessary to understand how God offers something outside ourselves (something objective) as a sure touchstone for our reckoning. To explain this concept further, we consider this predicament of Admiral Byrd and . . .

WHY HE NEEDED A TOUCHSTONE

YEARS AGO ADMIRAL BYRD DETERMINED to spend the winter near the South Pole for the purpose of scientific exploration. His fellow officers prepared for him a hut made of steel, entrenched in the ice and snow, buried beneath the icecap of Ross Barrier deep in Antarctica. They then left their chief alone, returning to Little America, an island 123 miles away. He was the only living human south of latitude seventy-eight. Blizzards roared above his hut and the temperatures plunged to eighty-two degrees below zero; he was completely surrounded by unending night. In his book, *Alone*, he explains how two different crises almost paralyzed him.

One day, the admiral left his hut to take a brisk walk in the harsh air. As he hiked, he suddenly wheeled about, horrified. He had gone too far! Absolutely nothing of his hut was visible. Stars in that polar night were hidden by heavy clouds. A white blanket of snow covering vast depths of ice was the only visible element. His footprints, the only guideposts to his hut, were lost in the shifting snow. He realized in an instant the graveness of his danger.

Were he to strike out in search of his hut and fail to hit upon it, all sense of direction would be lost; Byrd would be like a cork bobbing in mid-ocean. He would then only stumble about in the night of icy polar wastes to die. The possibility of tracking down his hut would be as slight as finding the proverbial needle in the haystack. What could he do?

Instead of giving way to panic, he had the presence of mind to understand he needed a FIXED TOUCHSTONE. Having with him a rod, he drove it into the ice and declared, "Here is my sure center!" The admiral knew a constantly moving axis was really no point of reckoning at all. So the rod became a fixed center of which he resolved not to lose sight. "I can always return to this rod," he thought, "for my hut cannot be far from it. By always keeping this pole in view, I'll not lose my way."

With rod in place, he struck out, groping in the darkness for some sight of his hut buried in the snow and ice. The admiral failed to see it in his first circle about, so he hurried back to his axis, the rod, of which he had not for a second lost sight. He started a second time, still confident, able to overcome fear because he had the fixed touchstone to which he clung with the resolve of a drowning man. The second and third attempts, however, were failures; his hut was as invisible as ever. The rod was still his only hope; just for a passing second, though, fear threatened to invade his soul as he realized the risk in extending the sphere of his quest. But expand it he must — he simply had to move out in a larger circle.

Then it happened! He explained that it was Providence; he was sure! There came a rift in the clouds and the stars burst upon his awful night. He could now increase the radius of his search, yet clearly keep his rod in view. So with the light of the stars aiding him, the admiral struck out once more into a wider sweep, further and further from his fixed point, all the while casting feverish glances toward his rod. And then miraculously his eyes fell upon his hut. He made one dive for the door almost hidden by the snow. He was home, safe from the perpetual darkness of the solar winter! It was the burst of light upon his rod serving as a proximate reckoning point that had led him home. Surely it was the intervening work of God to separate the clouds for a brief moment.

But there was still another crisis. One day the admiral discovered, to his horror, that he was slowly being poisoned by carbon monoxide escaping from his stove. What could he do? Isolated from all help, it would possibly take several months for anyone to reach him. Working feverishly to fix the stove and ventilation system, the fumes continued to seep, sending him in and out of consciousness. Byrd could not eat or sleep and eventually became so feeble that he could hardly leave his bunk. Almost convinced that he would die in his hut, he was afraid his body would be hidden forever by the unceasing snows.

What saved his life? In the depths of his despair, the admiral reached for his diary and tried to set down his philosophy of life — the absolute necessity of "linking oneself with the inexhaustible motive power that spins the universe." He thought of the stars overhead, of the orderly paths of the constellations and planets, and of how the everlasting sun would, in its time, return to lighten even the waste of the South Polar regions. And then while writing the words, "I am not alone," in his diary, a new surge of energy and hope filled his soul. Once again God had intervened.

This realization that he was not alone, not even in a hole in the ice at the end of the earth, was what saved Admiral Richard Byrd. "I know it pulled me through," he says. And he went on to add, "Few even in their lifetime come anywhere near exhausting the resources dwelling within them. There are deep wells of strength that are never used." His biographers suggest that Richard Byrd learned to tap that Well of Strength — as he turned to God.

WHAT IS GOD'S LESSON FOR US? God has planned that we need a reckoning point outside of ourselves — something objective — to which we can always look. God's word is that unchanging point, from one generation to the next. Though our life-experiences may change, we can always refer back to His word and measure by that standard. What the rod became for Admiral Byrd, the Word of God is for us.

GOD'S WORD EXPLAINS the passing over Jordan, *"that this may be a sign among you when your children ask in time to come, saying, 'What do these stones mean to you?'"* (Josh. 4:6 NKJV) They could then look to the twelve stones placed in the midst of the Jordan and the twelve stones placed outside of its banks as memorials. Though many years may have passed, they could reckon back to that point (those twelve stones) and announce, *"Israel came over this Jordan on dry land."* (Josh 4:22 KJV)

WE PRAY: Father, when the dark hours come, as they surely will, we have something more secure as our anchor, more sure than our feelings and circumstances. What the admiral learned we are likewise learning — Your Word is always our Rock.

There is a central message in the story of Jonah. What is God seeking to convey? Surely it is a merciful heart. Compare it with the self-centered prophet and see . . .

WHY JONAH HAS SO MANY CRITICS

ONE INTERVENTION IN SCRIPTURE that has called forth much unbelief and ridicule is the story of a runaway prophet who spent three days in the belly of a fish and lived to tell about it. The real issue is not between the doubter and this ancient record, but between the doubter and the Lord Jesus who authenticates it by comparing His own physical lodging in the grave to Jonah's three-day residence in the belly of the fish.

God's attribute of manifold mercy is foremost. God's sovereign control over nature and His exact timing is most obvious in these six amazing interventions by God:

- Jonah's calling to warn Nineveh of impending judgment,
- the storm that alerted the sailors to Jonah's running,
- the great fish maneuvered to rescue Jonah from the sea,
- the vine produced by God to shade the angry prophet,
- the worm prepared by God to destroy the vine, and
- the scorching wind that blows until Jonah is faint.

One must either accept these amazing interventions and the timing as directed by God, or refuse the whole story as a hoax. Once again we find our heart-attitude is exposed. We either want to believe God and His word or find reasons for rejecting it. Quite possibly there are some Jonahs reading this story now. Inwardly you have been aware of running from something God has asked of you. Now you are questioning — wondering why you are reaping certain consequences. Consider this question: Since you have been running, have you found yourself in a "storm" facing hopeless circumstances almost as impossible as Jonah's? Remember! There was hope for Jonah, but only as he repented.

Actually the story of Jonah is not so bizarre; it's not even unique. There are historical documentations of seafaring animals swallowing cows and horses and yes, even men. Some have actually retained their lives through the ordeal.

Sir Francis Fox records a story that he assures us was carefully investigated by two scientists, one of whom was N. Day Pardill, editor of a scientific journal in Paris. We share this excerpt from February 1891:

"The whale ship *Star of the East* was in the vicinity of the Falcon Islands, when the lookout spotted a large sperm whale three miles away. A boat was lowered, but the harpooners were unable to spear the whale in a short time. So a second boat attacked; it was upset by a lash of the whale's tail and the men were thrown into the sea. One man was drowned, and another, a James Bartley, disappeared and could not be found.

"When the whale was killed sometime later its great body was floating by the ship's side and the crew was busy with axes and spades removing the blubber. They worked all that day and into the night. The next morning they attached some tackle to the stomach which was hoisted onto the deck.

"The sailors were startled by spasmodic signs of life. Inside they found the missing sailor doubled up and unconscious. He was laid on the deck and treated to a bath of sea water which soon revived him, but his mind was not clear. He was placed in the Captain's quarters where he remained for two weeks, a raving lunatic. He was carefully treated by the Captain and officers of the ship until he gradually regained possession of his senses.

"At the end of the third week he had entirely recovered from shock and could resume his duties. During this sojourn in the whale's stomach, Bartley's skin was exposed to the strong action of the gastric juices and underwent a striking change. His face, neck, and hands were bleached to a deadly whiteness and took on the appearance of parchment. Bartley affirmed that he would probably have lived in this prison of flesh until he starved to death. He insisted he lost his senses from fright, not from loss of air."

But you know, there is one difference with that account. Jonah wasn't swallowed by a whale. The word in Hebrew is "dagh" which literally means a fish, not a whale or a mammal. Many suspect that the species of fish that swallowed Jonah was probably called a "Rhincodon typus," often called the "whale shark." Incidentally, Jacques Cousteau identified Rhincodons in the Mediterranean Sea.

Dr. Harry Rimmer, president of the Research Science Bureau, writes of an English sailor who was swallowed by a gigantic Rhincodon in the English Channel. Forty-eight hours after the accident occurred the fish was sighted and slain. The sailor was found unconscious on the inside, but still alive. He was rushed to a nearby hospital where he was declared to be suffering from shock alone, and a few hours later was released physically fit.

The man was put on exhibit in the London Museum at a shilling admittance fee, and billed as the "Jonah of the 20th Century." When Dr. Rimmer met this man personally he explained that his body was devoid of hair, and patches of a yellow-brown-whitish color covered his entire skin.

Our primary interest in the Biblical story is why did God continue to intervene in the life of Jonah? One thing we know — God desires to establish His merciful nature before men. Jonah himself explains this so well when he complained to the Lord, "This is exactly what I thought You'd do, Lord, when I was back in my own country and You first told me to come here. It was the reason I ran away to Tarshish. I knew You were a gracious God — merciful, slow to get angry, and full of kindness. I knew how easily You could cancel Your plans for destroying these people. (if they repented and changed their ways.) Self-centered Jonah pouted, "Please kill me, Lord; I'd rather be dead than alive (since nothing that I told them is happening)."

Then the Lord asked, "Is it right to be angry about this?"

Jonah then went out and sat sulking on the east side of the city. There God made a leafy shelter to shade him as he waited to see if anything would happen to the city.

WE ENTER INTO GOD'S BURDEN! God would have us recognize the amazing contrast between His merciful heart and the unmerciful prophet.

God was not willing that any should perish, while Jonah was eager to maintain his image and reputation (even if it meant destroying Nineveh). Father/God was compassionate toward 120,000; these persons are described as children who could not

discern their right hand from their left in Jonah 4:11. Jonah only felt sorry for himself when his shelter was destroyed — even though he did not work to put it there.

WE PRAY: FATHER/GOD I ask for a merciful heart like Yours, not cold or indifferent to the needs of others as your servant Jonah. I ask for a willingness to accept any assignment from You, even when it interferes with my plans or ignores my personal feelings about certain undeserving "Ninevites" You love. I want always to "stand with You" in weeping over lost humanity that needs to repent and acknowledge Your Lordship.

_____

_____

_____

_____

_____

_____

_____

_____

_____

_____

_____

_____

_____

_____

_____

_____

It was imperative that God should honor the sacrificial labors and dedication of His servants. For centuries the Enemy had held sway over the Maltos people. Now, the hour had come for God to sovereignly intervene and prove His faithfulness.

WHY THE FILM SPOKE TO THEM

SEVERAL YEARS AGO, a young missionary couple felt the call of God to take the gospel to a very resistant people in India known as the Maltos. With their young child, they moved to live in an area with the infamous moniker, "graveyard of missionaries." There they devotedly served the Lord; however, there was no receptivity among the people to whom they were trying to minister. Sharing the gospel seemed to fall on deaf ears often even generating hostility. Emotionally struggling through despair and physically facing obstacles such as polluted water, sickness was a constant companion.

One day after experiencing severe pain, the husband suddenly keeled over and died. It was a crisis for which his devastated wife was totally unprepared. But there was still more. Checking on their sick child, she discovered he also had died. Overwhelmed, confused, and suffering an acute sense of double loss, she left the mission field and returned to her home area in the South.

Not long afterwards, a team with governmental approval traveled into the same challenging area to show the *JESUS* film. Now, if you have seen the *JESUS* film, you know there is a very moving scene when Jesus is revealed at His baptism in the Jordan River. The moment Jesus' face emerged on the screen, the crowd vocally erupted. Forced to stop the movie, the team inquired about all of the commotion.

"It's Him, it's Him!" the people shouted. They could not believe what they were seeing. "We saw this same Man walking in the clouds!"

The team was astonished at their testimony. It seemed that everyone had seen the same vision of a huge man walking over the clouds while crying; this vision had appeared on the very same day that the missionary and his son had died. Believing this to be a message from the missionary's God, the Maltos people inferred from it that He was unhappy with them for rejecting the missionary's message; yet here through this film they were being given another opportunity.

The team was stunned. Resuming the movie presentation, the once agitated crowd calmed down. Everyone was transfixed by the story and when the service ended, the majority of those hostile, defiant Maltos trusted in Christ.

The Lord worked additional miracles as many experienced deliverance from evil spirits and still others were healed. The people's deep spiritual emptiness was filled. But there was a greater miracle yet! In an area where there were once no Christians at all, there are now tens of thousands of believers and hundreds of active churches. Today plans are underway by the Maltos to send out their own missionaries to unregenerate people groups; and because of its power, they too will use the *JESUS* film. What was once called the "graveyard of missionaries" has now become a "vineyard of missionaries."

WE CAN SHARE IN THEIR BURDEN: We realize that millions have prayed around the world for this film as it has gone to many

unreached peoples. A "corn of wheat has been planted" . . . and God has been reaping a harvest in His own way.

What can we expect in the future? God can do a "quick work" when certain conditions are met. Is it possible the hour is ahead when the "latter rain" will fall upon ripe harvest fields in every corner of the world . . . and we shall see millions come to Life in Him?

WE PRAY: Father, we are thankful that You allow us to enjoy a foretaste here and now of the powers of the future age. In this incident we have seen just a bit of Thy kingdom power demonstrated. We are eagerly awaiting that glorious hour when You will put on display for all the world to see — Your Son and all the family of sons who look like Him. Amen!

Adapted from The JESUS Film Project, http://www.jesusfilm.org/progress/special.html?type=regular&id=341

We must be convinced that we are involved in a cosmic battle which is supernatural, personal, and futile if fought with natural weapons. While we cannot fight Satan and his forces ourselves we can avail ourselves of the Lord's strength. As we acknowledge our weakness, we imitate Gideon's reduction from 32,000 warriors to 10,000 to 300, armed only with trumpets and lanterns (Judges 7). This divestment of natural strength enabled the putting on of God's power — and a mighty victory. In our day God is again <u>looking for spiritual warriors who will stand with Him through prayer</u>.

WHY GOD SENT A PROTECTIVE CLOUD

AS OUR PLANE REACHED A CERTAIN POINT, the friend sitting next to me said, "If you will look out the side window you will see the devastation caused by the second atomic bomb." Since I was American he felt sure it would have special interest to me . . . and it did.

While there had been much recovery work done, I could still see the ravages remaining from that direct hit which killed thousands and forever marred the landscape. I had not heard the amazing story of God's providential protection until newscaster Paul Harvey explained:

"One of America's mighty bombers took off from the island of Guam headed for Kokura, Japan, with a deadly cargo. Then a strange turn of events took place. Because clouds covered the target area, the sleek B-29 circled for nearly an hour until its fuel supply reached the danger point. The captain and his crew, frustrated because they were right over the primary target yet not able to fulfill their mission finally decided they had better go for the secondary target. Changing course, they found that the sky was clear. The command was given, "Bombs away!" and the B-29 headed for its home base.

"It was some time later an officer received startling information from military intelligence. Just one week before that bombing mission, the Japanese had transferred one of their largest concentrations of captured Americans to the city of Kokura. Upon reading this, the officer exclaimed, 'Thank God for that protecting cloud! If the city hadn't been hidden from the bomber, it would have been destroyed and thousands of American boys would have died.'"

Was that foggy cover, which rolled in from an otherwise sunlit sea, a mere happenstance? Hardly! By the way, that secondary target which I saw from my plane window was Nagasaki, and the deadly cargo intended for Kokura was the world's second atomic bomb. We are convinced that the concerted prayers of thousands of parents back in the USA enabled God to send forth that protective cloud cover.

God has often before used a protective cloud. Consider how in a most obvious way He led His people in their great exodus from Egypt. You will remember that miracle at the Red Sea which provided deliverance from the pursuing Egyptian army. It was that ever-present glory cloud which protected them as they passed through the waters. The same cloud remained over the camp to protect them from the desert sun — and to provide light at night.

HOW CAN WE SHARE HIS BURDEN: If we wonder why God so sovereignly intervenes, it is because the body of Christ is His unique

people. If we are annihilated by God's enemy, His purpose and plan cannot be fulfilled. But it is equally important that we each identify the spiritual battlefields in our lives today. Our God is looking for intercessors who understand the resources that are available. We do not fight for a position of victory, but we fight from a position already won at Calvary.

GOD'S WORD IS CLEAR: . . . *in the time of trouble He shall hide me . . .* (Psa. 27:5 NKJV) *One generation will commend your works to another. They will tell of Your mighty acts.* (Psa. 145:4 NIV)

WE PRAY: Father, it is our choice to stand with You in the place of a victory already won. We use that Name which is above all names to enforce the victory.

All nations of the world were stirred by the events of 9/11 when the Twin Towers fell. We know that was the work of our enemy; now we have come to recognize how God intervened to spare many lives which could have been lost. Consider these isolated events demonstrating God's work.

WHY GOD ORDERS OUR STEPS / STOPS

AT A MORNING MEETING the head of security summarized these stories of why certain people were still alive. Such trivial things intervened! Was this God sparing lives or was it chance? Read and find your own answer!

- The head of one company was late that day because he had to accompany his son to kindergarten.

- Another fellow was delayed because it was his turn to bring doughnuts.

- One woman was late because her alarm clock failed to ring.

- One fellow was late because of a traffic accident delay on the New Jersey turnpike.

- One individual had missed his bus, while another lady had spilled food on her clothes and needed to take extra time to change.

- One man's car wouldn't start, and another was delayed because he went back to answer the phone.

- One had a child who dawdled and was not ready when it was time to leave.

- Another explained that he had put on a new pair of shoes, but stopped at the drug store to buy a bandage when he developed a blister on his foot.

Consider this the next time you are stuck in traffic, miss an elevator or turn back to answer a ringing phone; those little things that annoy you could be your opportunity to rejoice in tribulations. However, we should not imply that every small event is ordered by God, for there are some interventions clearly sent by the Enemy.

Finally, the following story is told that is representative of so many other divine interventions on that particular day: "A few weeks before September 11th my wife and I found out we were going to have our first child. So, my wife planned a trip out to California to see her sister. On our way to the airport that morning we prayed that God would grant her a safe trip and be with her. Shortly after I said, 'Amen,' we both heard a loud pop and the car shook violently; we had blown a tire. I replaced the tire as quickly as I could but she still missed her flight. With much disappointment we returned home.

"As we reached our house I received a call from my father, an FDNY retiree. He asked what my wife's flight number was, but I explained that she had missed her flight. Then he informed me that her flight was the one which had crashed into the southern Twin Tower. I was too shocked to speak. My father also had more news for me; he was going to help the other firemen. 'This is not something I can just sit by for,' he explained, 'I have to do something.'

"I was concerned for his safety, of course, but more so because he had never given his life to Christ. After a brief debate on the phone, I knew his mind was made up. Before he got off the phone, he said, 'Take good care of my grandchild.' Those were the last words I ever heard my father speak. He died while helping in the rescue effort. My joy that my prayer for my wife had been answered quickly became anger — at God, at my father and at myself. I spent nearly two years blaming God for taking my father away. My son would never know his grandfather, my father had never trusted Christ and I never got to say good-bye.

"Then one day something wonderful happened. I was at home with my wife and son when we received a phone call from a man asking my father's name. Upon hearing it, he quickly exclaimed, 'I never got the chance to meet your father, but it is an honor to talk to his son.'

"He explained to me that his wife had worked in the World Trade Center and had been caught inside after the attack. She was pregnant and had been trapped in the debris. He then explained that my father had been the one to find his wife and free her. My eyes welled with tears as I thought of my father giving his life for these people. He then said, 'There is something else you need to know. As your father worked to free her, she talked to him and led Him to trust Christ.' I began sobbing at the news. What wonderful knowledge that when we get to heaven my father will be standing beside Jesus to welcome me, and this family would be able to thank him themselves!

"When their baby was born, they named him in honor of the man who gave his life so mother and baby could live."

It is amazing how God leaves His fingerprints in so many unusual ways. God spared these two mothers and their babies.

WE PONDER HIS WAYS: God's providence is that foresight and arrangement in advance of actual happenings by which God accomplishes the ends He has purposed beforehand. We do not understand all the "whys" but we can trust our Father who knows.

GOD'S WORD: *The mind of man plans his way, but the Lord directs his steps.* (Prov. 16:9 NASB)

WE PRAY: Father, we know the days of our years are numbered by Your providence. We cling to these words from Job, Though He slay me, yet will I trust Him. (Job 13:15 NKJV)

We look into the life of David Brainerd, a man wholly dedicated to reaching the heathen. History records how much his abandonment and passionate zeal affected those he touched. In this amazing incident we see how God intervenes to protect and use one yielded vessel who is available and adjustable.

WHY HE WAS SO EFFECTIVE

DAVID BRAINERD WAS A MAN with one great longing — to know Christ and to make Him known. When he moved alone into the depths of the forests to reach tribes of Indians he was often unable to speak their language. His friends marveled at his passionate zeal but felt sure they would never see him again.

After many hours of walking one day, he reached a new Indian tribe, pitched his tent and waited for the morning. He lingered in his tent that next morning praying and pleading with God to help him share the gospel with these savage Indians.

David assumed no eye but God was upon him, but the Indians had been scouting as he pitched his tent. They hastened back to their chief and told him of the approaching white man. A council among the braves was held; it was determined that the white invader must die! Returning to hide overnight in a sheltered place, the scouts monitored the little tent, waiting for him to appear.

But Brainerd delayed as he continued long in prayer. Finally the Indians became impatient; silently they drew near the tent to peer inside. Brainerd was on his knees. As they watched with utter amazement, a great rattlesnake pushed its ugly head under the tent wall and crawled toward the praying man. When the snake reached Brainerd, it reared itself as if to strike its fangs into the back of the missionary's neck. Then suddenly . . . it drew back! The braves puzzled . . . why did it glide out of the tent?

The watching braves were so amazed! Convinced that surely some unseen hand had kept that snake from injuring the white man, they rushed back to their village and explained to the chief what had happened. It seemed quite evident that the white man was under the protection of the Great Spirit; therefore, they must not harm him, but instead sue for peace.

Meanwhile, Brainerd finished his intercession, took his Bible and moved forward to the Indian village. To his surprise the whole tribe came out to greet him. With unusual respect they honored him and listened when he told them of Christ (he apparently found someone who could translate). They heeded his admonition to trust in Christ alone for salvation. Why not? How could they resist one who had been sent to them by the Great Spirit? This was one great victory for God . . . and for the Indians (though it was typical of God's interventions among them).

Since that time each generation that has learned about Brainerd's total abandonment has marveled at God's working through a man of such life-purpose. When A.J. Gordon gave this sketch of Brainerd's experience, he explained, "In order to speak to the Indians, it was necessary to find somebody who could even vaguely interpret his thoughts. Brainerd knew how absolutely dependent he was. So he spent whole days in prayer asking for the power of the Holy Spirit to come down so unmistakably that these Indians would not be able to stand before him. Once as he preached, we are told, the interpreter was so intoxicated he could hardly stand, yet God worked and scores were converted through this sermon."

William Carey read Brainerd's life-story and was so moved by it that he became a missionary to India. When Henry Martyn read about Brainerd's abandonment to God, the impact was so great he, too, went to India. We are told that Payson, missionary to China, read it as a young man of twenty; he confessed that he had never been so impressed by anything in his life. Jonathan Edwards gives his own testimony that knowing Brainerd personally changed his life.

HOW CAN WE ENTER INTO GOD'S BURDEN? It is no longer a secret! To be fruitful for God, as David Brainerd, is to demonstrate total abandonment to God, to demonstrate how genuinely we love Him and seek to be used by Him. Even as I write these words, my heart is strangely moved. I recall a similar challenge given to D. L. Moody — words which transformed his ministry. He heard a preacher announce: ". . . the world has yet to see what God will do through one man who is wholly yielded to Him." Sitting in the barn hayloft that afternoon, young Moody's heart responded to that call of the Spirit. He determined right then to be that man who would shake his generation. We all know the rest of the story.

TO KNOW GOD AND HIS WAYS IS IMPERATIVE: He is righteous in that He always does the right thing. Because He is good His actions are always consistent with His nature of love. (Ps. 119:137) *He is the Rock, His work is perfect; for all His ways are justice, a God of truth and without injustice; righteous and upright is He." (Deut. 32:4 NKJV)*

OUR PRAYER BURDEN is that many will share in the concern of Brainerd to reach the lost, even at great sacrifice. Father, there are folk I know all around me who need to hear the challenge, as did D.L. Moody, and respond.

Why is there such animosity when anyone attempts to resist abortion or homosexuality? It is because the enemy is dedicated to thwarting our Father/God's eternal purpose to have a family for His pleasure. We dare not fight this battle with carnal means but with spiritual warfare as we see demonstrated in . . .

WHY THE FLAG WAS SPARED

A FEW YEARS BACK the government of Tasmania (an island state of Australia) enacted legislation at the will of the vast majority, outlawing homosexual activity. Then the federal government of Australia was pressured by influential lobby groups who sought to veto Tasmania's new law through legislation of their own.

On the day this legislation was debated in the federal government, a large company of concerned people gathered to prayerfully demonstrate against such an amoral and sinful determination. It was evident the government was indifferent to the ideals of the people it served; they were simply reacting to please a vocal minority.

Hank Massen explains what happened. "We peacefully demonstrated outside the building, praying for lost souls inside, worshipping and singing unto the Lord. Then the police — unthinking servants of the state — began to violently quell the demonstration. As they attacked us we peacefully submitted, meeting their hate with love, even as Jesus did with His foes.

"Suddenly a violent storm began to brew over the Parliament House, enveloping protestors and police alike, in a swirl of sharp rain and biting hail. As the police fled screaming, our group serenely fell to our knees, knowing this was indeed a sign from the Lord for which we had prayed. We continued to cry out to God for Him to direct our actions.

"The storm cloud was the color of a livid bruise — purple and dark — such a cloud formation as never seen before in Canberra. As I opened my eyes for a moment, ignoring the wind and rain, I saw the cloud roll back from the sky's center, creating a large hole. From this center burst forth a mighty bolt of lightning illuminating the whole area around.

"The Parliament House of Australia has a large flagpole with the Australian flag flying atop the roof; the flag consists of six stars representing the six states. This burst of lightning, directed by God Himself, struck the flag almost completely destroying it. But as we stood in wonder at what was happening, a small segment of the flag — the only remaining part of it — floated to the feet of our group on a gentle wind.

"It was the star of Tasmania, whole and unblemished by the intense heat that had destroyed the rest. To all of us it was a most obvious intervention by God — the star of Tasmania representing the only state that stood with God. Amazing!

"You can be sure the incident received little news coverage; indeed, only thirty seconds was shown at the end of the local news bulletin. It seemed obvious the frightened politicians had pled with the news media to keep this incident quiet."

Was God making some statement in this most sovereign intervention? Who can explain such obvious indignation! It was as though God said, "I've had enough!" His manifest anger will always oppose whatever thwarts or challenges His ultimate intention for a family. We can be sure our Heavenly Father will fulfill His purpose to conform a vast family of sons to the image of His firstborn Son, the Lord Jesus.

Homosexuality, abortion and infanticide...all of these represent Satan's master agenda to derail God's plan. It should not surprise us that Satan will focus his efforts on presenting a caricature of God — a false concept of our Father/God.

A.W. Tozer has warned, "There is a strong tendency among religious teachers these days to disassociate anger from the Divine character of God and to defend God by explaining away the 'wrath' scriptures that relate to Him. This is understandable, but in the light of the full revelation of God, it is inexcusable.

"In the first place," Tozer continues, "God needs no defense. Those teachers who are forever trying to make God over in their own image might better be employed in seeking to make themselves over in the image of God. The present refusal of so many to accept the doctrine of the wrath of God is a part of a larger pattern of unbelief that begins with doubt concerning the veracity of the Bible.

"Whatever is stated clearly but once in the Scriptures," Tozer concludes, "may be accepted as sufficiently well-established to invite the faith of all believers. And when we discover that the Spirit speaks of the wrath of God about 300 times in the Bible we may as well make up our minds to accept the doctrine or reject the Scriptures outright."

From Genesis on, Satan has directed his attack on corrupting the human race and thereby doing away with the Adamite stock through whom the seed of the woman should come. When the sons of God (fallen angels) married the daughters of men, producing giants, it was a frontal assault on God's plan for His family. So God sent the flood as a great correction! Besides His wrath there is always this other side of God's character which we need to see.

ANOTHER DIVINE IMPERATIVE: Did you ever consider why Methusaleh lived so long — 969 years? It is interesting how much prophetic insight God hides in the meaning of names. When Enoch begat his son, Methusaleh, the meaning in this name was "when he is dead it shall come." Many who interpret the Bible insist that the very day Methusaleh died, the flood began. Can you see the longsuffering of God? He extended his days and waited and waited in mercy before sending judgment upon all mankind. Yes, the God of wrath is also merciful and longsuffering — not willing that any should perish. But His "spirit will not always strive . . ."

Again, God's wrath and fiery intervention against Sodom was simply to expose and destroy homosexuality with all its consequences. How merciful God was to alert Abraham when He was about to send judgment upon Sodom. *"Shall I hide from Abraham what I am about to do?"* (Gen. 18:17 NIV)

WE PRAY: Father/God we are convinced You alerted the folk in Tasmania. Now, You are alerting our nation (and others around the globe) who practice homosexuality and abortion, of Your great displeasure. We join with Abraham in asking, "Will you destroy the righteous with the wicked?" Our only hope is that through intercession once again You will in mercy rescue the righteous remnant (yes, Lot's family) before Your wrath descends. Father, I ask that every young person reading this will honor Your fatherhood and Your purpose for a vast family of sons and daughters — all conformed to the image of the Pattern Man . . . our Lord Jesus. Give us wisdom and special grace to intervene — even as You intervene — to rescue those who are living carelessly without regard to the sure consequences of living selfishly. AMEN!

Sometimes a merciful God must deal in wrath. We are so accustomed to enjoying a God of love and compassion it is difficult to accept the other side of God's character. But it is necessary for us to recognize that a Father who truly loves His Son will be very jealous for His sacrificial work on Calvary. A demonstration of this is . . .

WHY GOD DEALT SEVERELY

IT WAS AN AWFUL TRAIN WRECK. Through an engineer's error the train had run past the small station onto an open switch and into the path of the oncoming express. Doctors and nurses rushed to the scene where many were dead and seriously injured. Mr. Waters, a passenger on the ill-fated train, had escaped injury and was moving about seeking to comfort the suffering victims.

As Mr. Waters knelt beside one of the dying passengers who was fatally hurt, he sought to reassure the dying man. But the man insisted that Mr. Waters listen to the following story, and tell it to others as a warning:

The man explained that ten years before, while traveling as a salesman for a firm, he had spent a night of revelry with friends in the bar of a hotel. That evening the conversation turned to ridicule of a gospel meeting being held in that town. An elderly preacher was proclaiming the good news of God's love to many attentive hearts. Several were responding, in fact some of the local drunks had been converted and gave testimony of their deliverance. This seemed to increase the hatred and enmity of the men who directed their scorn toward the servant of the Lord and all who showed interest in the meetings.

Mr. Waters listened attentively as the injured man continued his story. "On that particular night all kinds of wicked pranks were played, and the more my buddies and I drank, the worse they became. When someone questioned how the gospel meetings were conducted, a drunken young man offered to give a demonstration if the others would join him.

"Six of us kneeled on the floor, and started the mockery. We prayed for the forgiveness of our sins, and even tried to imitate tears of repentance. Then we closed with a song we had learned in childhood. 'Rock of Ages cleft for me . . .' When all of this was finished, we found ourselves alone in the bar. Shocked by the awful blasphemy, the rest of the patrons had left the room."

The injured passenger paused and then continued, "What I am about to tell you is not fiction; this is what has happened in the last ten years to those of us who participated in that farce. Before the end of the year, the hotel owner suffered a fall, which burst a blood vessel in his brain. He never regained consciousness before he died. Some might think this is not unusual, but notice . . . it was a violent death.

"Two years later the young man who started the demonstration was with a hunting party. During the night he got up to get a drink of water. In the dark he missed his way and fell down the steps, broke his neck and died two days later.

"The third was a very odd fellow named Tom, who in mockery cried out the loudest. Tom fell down his own cellar steps and died.

"Now," he continued, "I began to be uneasy. What would happen to my remaining companions? Fearfully, one of these went west hoping to avoid such a tragic end. I heard that he became a railway guard who got caught between the bumpers of two coaches and died a horrible death.

"Last year I met my only surviving companion. He had fallen into deep poverty after having lost his wife and two children. One evening he fell from the door of a bar onto the concrete walk. His head struck a rock that pierced his temple and he died instantly.

"Since that time I have waited for my end. I knew I could not escape it, and now it has come." He took a deep sigh and died.

AMAZING! In ten years each of the six men who took part in that blasphemy and mockery died violent deaths. As far as we know, not one of them had turned to God in repentance. Are we assuming too much to suggest that God is very jealous for His Son and His sacrificial death on the cross? I believe these untimely deaths were an intervention from God. It was His way of announcing "Don't mock the loving sacrifice of my Son on the cross!" Sometimes God speaks loudly! The apostle Paul writes in Romans 11:22 of ". . . *the goodness and severity of God . . ."* (KJV)

Throughout the scriptures and in our own observation of life we have seen the longsuffering and mercy of God toward all those who in repentance acknowledge their sinful conditon and trust Christt. But it is also evident that He is a God of wrath, who is very jealous for the sacrificial work of His Son on Calvary. (Consider our lesson in *Life's Ultimate Privilege* where we explain this jealousy more fully.)

I am well aware that it is the habit of the Christian pulpit today to downplay these subjects of wrath, severity and jealousy in God. Whoever tried to build a mega-church on such an unpopular message? If these attributes in God are even acknowledged it is with the briefest of mentions. However, God is still in control. He will very soon speak the last word of warning to this Laodicean church, *"I know thy works — repent!"*

HOW CAN WE ENTER INTO HIS BURDEN?Because there is similar mockery in our day, I would like to ask how your heart responds when you hear of these six men dying violent deaths? If there is some hidden area of resistance toward God's full will in your life, it is likely you feel that it wasn't fair! Perhaps you think that God should have given them another chance — more opportunity to repent. Possibly in some disguised manner your heart is prone to challenge God's ways.

Make no mistake — once our hearts have been truly conquered by God's love and compassion, we will be quick to respond, "I don't need to understand all God's ways . . . I will simply trust Him." Like Job, we will proclaim, *"Though He slay me, yet will I trust Him . . ."* (Job 13:15 NKJV)

It was evident in the nature of their religious mockery that each of these men was rejecting "light" they had previously received. One thing becomes very clear — it is most dangerous to lightly esteem or openly scorn Jesus' sacrifice for us on the cross.

FATHER, help me to recognize the condition of my heart. Keep me from allowing any subtle accusations of the Enemy when I might be puzzled about things I do not understand.

Here is the amazing survival story of a celebrated war hero who explains how God intervened. Stranded and facing a hopeless situation for more than twenty-one days on the Pacific Ocean, the crew recognized it was God's mercy when He responded to their cry of desperation

WHY HIS LIFE WAS CHANGED

CAPTAIN EDWARD RICKENBACKER WAS THE FEATURED SPEAKER at our Saturday night Youth for Christ rally in Salem, Oregon. The captain had recently returned home and now was on a speaking tour. When I picked him up at the hotel I looked forward, along with 1500 others, to hearing him explain how God had sovereignly intervened during the twenty-one days he was adrift on a raft.

Rickenbacker and his crew had left Hawaii by airplane for a certain island. During the flight their compass failed and their radio ceased to work properly. When they could find no place to land and their gas supply was exhausted, they were forced to crash into the treacherous waters of the Pacific.

In their haste to escape the airplane before it sank, they grabbed little in the way of supplies — only four oranges and three lifeboats. So they were eight men bobbing in three rubber rafts — three in one, three in another and two in the third boat all tied together so that they could encourage each other.

Private Bartek in the captain's boat had a Bible in the pocket of his jumpsuit, so the second day afloat they began prayer meetings. Each morning and evening the men took turns reading passages from the Bible.

The captain tenderly explained how during those heart-searching days, "we knew things about these men's lives that had never been expressed before — sins of commission or omission were openly confessed."

"Frankly," he declared to the audience, "we prayed, crying out to God for His deliverance. After the oranges were gone and hunger pangs gripped us, we asked God for food. If it weren't for the fact that I had seven witnesses, I wouldn't dare tell this story because it seems so fantastic.

"Within an hour after praying for food, a sea gull flew over and landed on my head. You can imagine my nervousness in trying to reach my hand around to get it, which I did. We wrung its neck and feathered it and carved the carcass, distributing it among us. Then using the remains as bait, we were able to catch two fish.

"When we ran into rain storms we caught water with our shirts, socks and handkerchiefs, wringing them out for drink. For several days this meant two sips of water per man. Thankfully the rain water increased during the last few days."

The thirteenth day brought a death, and one man was buried at sea. The seventeenth, eighteenth, and nineteenth days brought occasions when airplanes flew over, but the drifting men were not noticed.

On the twentieth day, the crew separated their rafts and floated apart. Captain Cherry was subsequently found in his boat alone. Three men in another raft had drifted to an uninhabited island to later be rescued. On the twenty-first day, Captain Rickenbacker and the two men in his boat were rescued by American planes.

Imagine how deeply the audience was moved by the captain's testimony and the evident change in a man who was now living with a new sense of destiny. Yet I could sense that after being on a two-month tour sharing about this miraculous deliverance he was very weary.

As we drove to his hotel that night I asked him how many times he had presented this message. He quickly replied, "Too many times!" As I recall, it was nearly a hundred times. He was not inclined for more conversation, so I dropped him off realizing I was "just another person running taxi for him."

Since that time more than fifty-five years have passed and I, myself, have enjoyed traveling as a speaker. It has been my opportunity to challenge people to cry out to God in their own times of desperation – and to explain that He is not some distant God in the far-off heavens. He is our Father — who is always available.

BUT I DO HAVE THIS BURDEN: How can we keep our message fresh and relevant to the hearts who are listening? Certainly it's not through repeating someone else's account, such as the amazing story told by the captain; somehow we must maintain freshness in sharing <u>our own</u> testimonies. Is there some secret?

I have concluded that if we are determined in our message to exalt the Lord Jesus, then God will give anointing for freshness. When our goal is to always place Him in the highest position of honor, God will be pleased to anoint.

After His death and resurrection our Lord Jesus was exalted to sit at the Father's right hand. There is one proof that Jesus is seated there in the heavenlies at the Father's right hand — the Holy

Spirit has been poured forth upon believers. This can be a WONDERFUL INTERVENTION into our daily living! Yes, it is because the Lord Jesus has been exalted to the throne that the Father has poured forth an anointing. In reading Psalm 133 we discover the anointing that was first poured upon the head (Aaron's) then reached down to the body (of which we are a part). If you want freshness in your message, exalt the Lord Jesus.

GOD'S WORD IS CLEAR: *"Therefore having been exalted to the right hand of God, and having received from the Father the promise of the Holy Spirit, He has poured forth this which you both see and hear."* (Acts 2:33 NASB)

WE PRAY: Father, I do understand how much You desire the exaltation of the Lord Jesus. Let this be my constant aim.

The book, *Eternity in Their Hearts*, reveals how God has long been intervening in people groups. This amazing incident will enlarge your vision of God's faithfulness in bringing the light to those in heathen darkness.

WHY A PONY LED THEM TO THE BOOK

DON RICHARDSON EXPLAINS HOW for many centuries God has been intervening in people groups throughout the world, seeking to turn them from darkness to light. His book, *Eternity in Their Hearts*, will surely enlarge your vision of God's faithfulness. This amazing incident illustrates how sovereignly God works even in heathen darkness.

About 100,000 tribesmen called the Wa were headhunters who once a year felt compelled by bloodthirsty gnats to plant human heads in their fields along with seeds — just to ensure a good crop, mind you! They really didn't want to hurt anyone; they just wanted a good crop. One can recognize why neighboring tribes always wished to leave for vacation when Wa were planting their crops; unfortunately that was when they had to plant their crops, too.

But a benign influence was at work within the folk religion of the Wa. From time to time prophets of the true God, called Siyeh by the Wa, arose to condemn headhunting and spirit appeasement. One such prophet, PuChan, appeared during the 1880s, persuading several thousand Wa tribesmen to abandon headhunting. PuChan said that the true God, Siyeh, was about to send a long-awaited "white brother with a copy of the lost book." If he came close to Wa territory and discovered that the Wa were practicing evil things, he might think them unworthy of the true God-book and turn away from them again! If this happened, PuChan warned, surely the Wa would never get another chance to have the lost book restored to them.

One morning PuChan saddled a Wa pony. "Follow this pony," he said to some of his disciples. "Siyeh told me last night that the white brother has finally come near! Siyeh will cause this pony to lead you to him. When you find the white brother, let him mount this pony. We would be ungrateful people if we made him walk the last part of his journey toward us."

While PuChan's disciples gaped in astonishment, the pony started walking. Expecting the pony to stop at the nearest stream, they followed it. Would it lead them to the "white brother bearing the book of Siyeh, the true God?"

The pony led those amazed disciples over approximately 200 miles of mountainous trails and down into the city of Kentung. Then it turned into the gate of a mission compound and headed straight for a well. The pony stopped beside the well. PuChan's disciples looked in all directions, but could see no trace of either a white brother or a book.

Explaining what happened next is Nelda Widlund, daughter of Vincent Young and granddaughter of William Marcus Young; she was raised on that very mission compound and drank often from that well. The details which follow form a treasured memory for the entire Young clan.

The Wa tribesmen heard sounds in the well. They looked inside it and saw no water, but only two clear blue eyes looking up at them out of a friendly, bearded white face. "Hello strangers!" The voice, speaking in their language, echoed out of the well. "May I help you?" William Marcus Young climbed out of the well (which he was in the process of digging).

As he brushed the dust from his hands and faced them, the Wa messengers asked, "Have you brought a book of God?" Young nodded yes. The Wa men, overcome with emotion, fell at his feet and blurted out their message from PuChan. They insisted, "This pony is saddled especially for you. Our people are all waiting. Fetch the book! We must be on our way back to our people."

Young stared at them. "I can't leave," he painfully explained, "Thousands of Lahu come here almost daily for teaching. They are wholly dependent upon me. What shall I do?"

Young presented the situation to the Lahu Christians. Together they decided to provide accommodations for the Wa men so that they, too, could receive teaching and make trips back into Wa territory to teach their own people. By this means PuChan and thousands of his people became Christians without a single visit from William Marcus Young!

Later, Vincent Young, youthful grandson, made repeated journeys into the Wa mountains — an area avoided by travelers because of the Wa reputation for headhunting — and provided more detailed teaching "on location." A New Testament translation for the Wa people followed, and 10,000 baptized Wa converts helped spread the gospel still further into eastern Burma and southwestern China.

Some day when we all gather in eternity and witness the multitudes of redeemed from every tribe we will be amazed how much God has been working throughout these people groups — long before missionaries even arrive. It is difficult for us to imagine how one of their heathen prophets received direction from God — urging them to seek for HIS BOOK! But they did!

HERE IS ANOTHER DIVINE IMPERATIVE: that God would prove His love for the heathen; He is jealous in His desire that His word be available to all. . . . *No prophecy of the scripture is of any private interpretation, for the prophecy came not in old time by the will of man, but holy men of God, spake as they were moved by the Holy Ghost.* **(2 Pet. 1:20-21 KJV)**

Our God, who so loved the world, is continually making every overture to reach out and awaken those who live in darkness. He has already spoken His word into the pages of His book, and now waits for His servants to make it available everywhere. How concerned He is for **THIS BOOK**, and He zealously watches over those who become ambassadors carrying such good news. To really know how God values His word, let us join with the Psalmist in this exaltation. (We use this translation for a fresh look)

The revelation of God is whole and pulls our lives together.

The signposts of God are clear and point out the right road.

The life-maps of God are right, showing the way to joy.

The directions of God are plain and easy to the eyes.

God's reputation is twenty-four carat gold, with a lifetime guarantee.

The decisions of God are accurate down to the nth degree.

God's Word is better than a diamond,

better than a diamond set between emeralds.

You'll like it better than strawberries in spring,

better than red, ripe strawberries.

There's more: God's Word warns us of danger

and directs us to hidden treasure.

Otherwise how will we find our way?

or know when we play the fool? (Psalm 19:7-11 Msg)

WE PRAY: Father/God we bow in gratitude before You. The more we know of the great price You paid in giving Your own Son to reconcile all men to Yourself, the more we're constrained to bow in humble adoration. Every time You intervene in our affairs it is another expression of Your loving concern. We continue to marvel at the livingness of Your Word, and that it will daily "direct us to hidden treasure." Amen!

Adapted from *Eternity in Their Hearts*, by Don Richardson

No one can ignore the intelligent design in God's natural realm, for His fingerprints are manifest everywhere. God's intervention is so evident in each level of creation as we shall see in this lesson. What the animal world does by instinct, mankind does by choice. Those of us who have a heart to appreciate and eyes to see are quick to acknowledge . . .

WHY GOD'S GLORY IS IN ALL CREATION

AS A BOY GROWING UP ON THE PRAIRIES of South Dakota, I often watched geese as they departed for warmer climates to escape the cold north and icy harshness of the coming winter. It was hard to for me to understand why they were flying in a "V" formation, but I later learned that when the leader would drop back from leading, another would take his place at the point of the "V." I also learned that in their long journey the formation would appear erratic and disjointed at times. A stricken goose would plummet earthward leaving a gaping hole in the ranks. Responding instantly, two flanking geese would track their fallen comrade and, with agility, drop to his aid. As the main flock would continue its southward migration, the two loyal birds would remain at the side of the wounded brother until he was fully restored to health . . . or dead.

Amazing! It is the instinctive nature that God has built into them for preservation. Geese cannot articulate their reasons for breaking ranks at their own peril to station themselves beside a crippled, wounded fellow. But they seem driven by an innate urgency to respond to a companion's desperate situation. What geese do by instinct, we as members of the Body of Christ ought to do by choice.

One day while driving on a rural road in South Dakota, I saw a pheasant sitting in the middle of the road. With no time to swerve, I drove right over it. Stopping to look back, I assumed the bird was surely dead; to my amazement, however, it was still alive although it remained exactly in the same place. With curiosity I walked back to see if the bird was wounded. No — but under its wings were six or eight little chicks, which the mother hen continued to protect even as I stood observing. Why? It was instinct built into its mothering nature. Yes, it was God's fingerprints demonstrating His glory in creation.

Some time back, the front page of the *San Francisco Chronicle* printed a story about a female humpback whale that had become entangled in a web of crab traps weighing hundreds of pounds, causing her to struggle to stay afloat. She also had hundreds of yards of line-rope wrapped around her body, her tail, her torso, and in her mouth.

When a fisherman spotted her east of the Farallon Islands outside the Golden Gate, he radioed an environmental group for help. Soon the rescue team arrived and determined the whale was so entrapped the only way to save her would be to dive in and cut the ropes ... a very dangerous proposition, for one slap of the tail could kill a rescuer.

After working for hours with curved knives they eventually freed her. Immediately when she realized she was free, the divers say she swam in what seemed like joyous circles. She then came back to each and every diver, one at a time; nudging them by pushing gently around them, she thanked them. Some said it was the most incredibly beautiful experience of their lives. The man who cut the rope out of her mouth says her eye carefully followed him the whole time, and he will never be the same.

Amazing! We know that God has designed mankind with a deep need (and desire) to express thankfulness. Was this whale also demonstrating thankfulness in the only way she could? Yes, we are convinced that even animals have this inner need to express thankfulness as well.

It seems to us that the Psalmist is enthralled with God's handiwork, which not only reveals God's existence but also demonstrates His glory (satisfaction).

GOD'S WORD (PSALM 19) DECLARES:

The revelation of God is whole and pulls our lives together.

The signposts of God are clear and point out the right road.

The life maps of God are right, showing the way to joy.

The directions of God are plain and easy on the eyes. (vs. 7-8 Msg)

YES WE CAN ENTER INTO HIS BURDEN: One look at the final chapters of the book of Revelation reveals that all creation will spend the coming ages in thanksgiving, praise and worship. Since this is our heavenly calling, it is imperative that we be prepared and that we help others become prepared for life's ULTIMATE OCCUPATION — WORSHIP!!!

- **Prayer is the soul's occupation with its needs.**

- **Praise is the soul's occupation with its blessings.**

- **Worship is the soul's occupation with its God.**

WE PAUSE FOR WORSHIP: Father, we have just discovered that You will be sponsoring a great celebration to which we are invited. According to scripture, those allied with the Lamb of God will join with the heavenly choir in shouting, "Hallelujah!" How glorious that the voices of many redeemed will extol Your salvation, glory and power.

The God who at times has sovereignly intervened will now be INTERVENING FOREVER AND FOREVER. AMEN!

WE PRAY! With hearts full of gratitude we bow in humble adoration . . . and acknowledge . . . YOU are worthy to receive!

_____

_____

_____

_____

_____

_____

_____

_____

_____

_____

_____

_____

_____

_____

_____

_____

_____

In his autobiography, a well-known TV personality describes the time when he asked, "If God the Father is so all-loving, why didn't <u>He</u> come down and go to Calvary?" His comment reveals that he really did not understand much about our Father.

WHY GOD INTERVENED

JOHN STOTT DESCRIBES . . . at the end of time, millions of people were scattered on a great plain before God's throne. Some of the groups near the front talked heatedly, not cringing with shame but with belligerence.

"How can God judge us? How can He know about suffering?" snapped a brunette. She jerked back a sleeve to reveal a number from a Nazi concentration camp. "We endured terror, beatings, torture and death!"

In another group, a black man lowered his collar. "What about this?" he demanded, showing an ugly rope burn. "We suffocated in slave ships, were wrenched from our loved ones, and toiled until only death gave release."

Far out across the plain were hundreds of such groups. Each had a complaint against God for the evil and suffering He had permitted in His world. How lucky God was to live in heaven where all was sweetness and light, where there was no weeping, no fear, no hunger, no hatred; indeed, what did God know about what man had been forced to endure in this world? After all, God lead a pretty sheltered life, they said.

So each group sent out a leader, chosen because he had suffered the most. There was a Jew, a black, an Indian untouchable, an illegitimate, a Hiroshima victim, and a Siberian slave camp refugee. In the center of the plain, they consulted with each other.

At last they were ready to present their case. It was rather simple; before God would be qualified to be their judge, He must endure as they had. Their decision was that God "should be sentenced to live on earth — as a man." But, because He was God, they set certain safeguards to be sure He could not use His divine powers to help Himself.

- Let Him be born a Jew.
- Let the legitimacy of His birth be doubted, so that none would know who was truly His father.
- Let Him champion a cause so just, but so radical, that it would engender towards Him the hate, condemnation, and elimination efforts of every major traditional and established religious authority.
- Let Him try to describe what no man has ever seen, tasted, heard or smelled — let Him try to communicate God to men.
- Let Him be betrayed by His dearest friends.
- Let Him be indicted on false charges, tried before a prejudiced jury and convicted by a cowardly judge.
- Let Him see what it was like to be terribly alone and completely abandoned by every living thing.
- Let Him be tortured and then let Him die! Let Him die a humiliating death, with common thieves.

As each leader announced his portion of the sentence, loud murmurs of approval went up from the great throng of people. When the last had finished pronouncing sentence, there was a long silence

No one moved — for suddenly all knew . . . God had already served His sentence. (J.S.)

. . . and there was silence in heaven about the space of half an hour."
(Rev. 8:1 KJV)

FATHER, we can trust You. There is no other thing that we can say; You have proved to us that You are worthy!

Adapted from "The Silence," *The Cross of Christ*, by kind permission of John Stott, InterVarsity Press

MAINTAINING OUR SHARPER FOCUS

Offering another prayer journal is one way of alerting you — our burden is to call forth a remnant of spiritual prayer warriors who will dedicate themselves to a vital partnership in fulfilling His purpose in the closing hours of this age.

Every day we are hearing from you. We rejoice! In spite of your personal battles, you have made yourselves available for others. One realtor, who freely shares books, phoned to tell me about a lady who had just finished reading one of our books. He passed the phone to her and I listened as she joyfully explained how God had used a lesson to speak to her. My heart was lifted up with thanksgiving.

Then as he finished our phone conversation, he quietly added, "You know, our sister here is 103 years old! What a delight she is!" I thought to myself that yes, our bodies might feel their age, but "our spirits can be forever-young" when we are joined to His Spirit.

Today I make this plea! Most everyone is too preoccupied with things that seem important – yet are not. I remember the exhortation my mother so often gave me in my early years when I was troubled; she said again… and again, "What difference will it make next year?" She was demonstrating her sharper focus in the light of eternity – which is something we all need.

WE MEET YOU DAILY AT HIS THRONE
DeVern & Ruth

OTHER BOOKS BY DEVERN FROMKE

Life's Ultimate Privilege

This fifteen day journey has become a favorite. Many churches and study groups have used these lessons to stimulate personal and corporate growth. Now over 210,000 copies in a short time demonstrate both the challenge and value of this devotional book.

The Larger Window

This selection of 100 amazing stories will demonstrate how God can move each of us from being objects of grace, mercy and peace to BECOME channels and models to bless others. While the stories are both entertaining and challenging, the author has one definite goal: to move each of us from our preoccupation with what we can get from God to what He will get as we become wholly alive unto Him for fulfilling His purpose.

The Ultimate Intention

This classic has been revised with a study guide for those who desire class participation. For more than 40 years DeVern Fromke's writings have emphasized the God-centered view of reality as imperative for our vision and growth. It is no exaggeration to say that this volume has radically altered the ministry of many key leaders in this country and around the world. Now over 200,000 copies and in many languages, this volume will move every reader from a self-center to God-centeredness.

Unto Full Stature

This newly revised volume unveils very practical outworking of the Ultimate truth. The author attempts to lead each one step by step through eight levels or phases of our natural and spiritual maturity. He exposes hidden reasons why the child of God flounders in spiritual perspective, often disregards the place of the will and too often abuses his body as he zealously lives at exhaustion point. Many churches have used this with classroom participation.

PRAYER JOURNALS NOW AVAILABLE
The purpose of each journal is to sharpen your focus —
. . . to become more effective in prayer/intercession

Lord, help us to recognize each . . .
DOOR OF OPPORTUNITY
TO PARTNER WITH HIM
TO BECOME HIS VOICE
TO REPRESENT HIM
TO CELEBRATE HIS GRACE
TO KNOW HIM

FATHER IS LOOKING FOR THOSE . . .
WHO WILL STAND WITH HIM
WHO ARE AVAILABLE
WHO WILL STAND IN THE GAP
WHO WILL LISTEN
WHO HAVE A SINGLE EYE
WHO BEAR HIS IMAGE

WHY . . . GOD INTERVENES OH . . . I UNDERSTAND
WHY A DAY WAS MISSING
WHY HEZEKIAH'S PRAYER WAS WRONG
WHY GOD SENT A WINDOW
WHY GOD SENT THE DOVE
WHY A PONY LED THEM
WHY GOD SENT A CLOUD
WHY THE SWIM COACH SAW A CROSS
WHY THE TASMANIA FLAG WAS SPARED
WHY GOD PROVIDED A WALL (& 11 OTHERS)

I am grateful for their help:

. . . to DeVon for servicing our computers,

. . . to Michele for her diligence and wisdom in helping edit this manuscript

. . . my wife, Ruth — who is God's Gracious Gift to me, always helpful, discerning exactly what needs to be done.

. . . I give my thanks…but even more importantly:

THE LORD IS PLEASED WITH YOUR LABOR.